MW00337716

IN ORDINARY LIGHT

LOUISIANA WRITERS SERIES

IN ORDINARY LIGHT

New and Selected Poems

DARRELL BOURQUE

University of Louisiana at Lafayette Press
2010

Author Photograph: Philip Gould
Cover Art Photograph: Philip Gould

Cover Art by Karen Bourque:
Bayou Plaquemine Brûlée Dyptich
l) Persimmon with Egret   2) Persimmons by Moonlight

http://ulpress.org
University of Louisiana at Lafayette Press
P.O. Box 40831
Lafayette, LA 70504-0831

ISBN 13 (paperback): 978-1-935754-01-5

Printed on acid-free paper in Canada.

Library of Congress Cataloging-in-Publication Data

Bourque, Darrell.
  In ordinary light : new and selected poems / Darrell Bourque.
    p. cm. -- (Louisiana writers series)
  Includes bibliographical references.
  ISBN 978-1-935754-01-5 (pbk. :alk. paper)
  I. Title.
  PS3602.O89275I5 2010
  811'.6--dc22
                        2010038687

For Karen,
always

CONTENTS

IN ORDINARY LIGHT

NEW POEMS

2004–2009

I

II

III

From *PLAINSONGS*

1994

From *THE DOORS BETWEEN US*

1997

&

From *BURNT WATER SUITE*

1999

From *BURNT WATER SUITE*

1999

THE BLUE BOAT

Complete

2004

I

II

III

From *CALL AND RESPONSE: CONVERSATIONS IN VERSE*

with Jack B. Bedell

2009

From ***Holding the Notes***

Forthcoming, 2011

(with special permission from Chicory Bloom Press)

Acknowledgments

I would like to express gratitude to the presses, editors, and journals below that have published versions of many of these poems. I extend special thanks to the teachers, mentors, and readers who have guided my work over the years: Van K. Brock, Luis Urrea, Ann Dobie, Sheryl St. Germain, Barry Ancelet, Gloria Fiero, Michael Sartisky, Jack B. Bedell, and Reggie Young. I am especially grateful to the writers of the Acadiana Writing Project for whom I have led many workshops and with whom I have written for many years, as well as writers in the other Louisiana Writing Project workshops with whom I have worked over the years. I am also grateful to Beverly Matherne of Northern Michigan University and to the NMU graduate and undergraduate writers in the 2004 workshop, as well as to the University of Louisiana at Lafayette, the staff of the Center for Louisiana Studies, Leslie Donahue Schilling of ULL's Humanities Resource Center, and the University's Friends of the Humanities who have sustained and supported my work over the years. I am grateful to Christine Balfa Powell for her translation work in *Plainsongs* and to Barry Ancelet who has been a French language consultant, translator, and resource for many of the poems appearing in this collection. I am grateful to the directors and staff of University of Louisiana at Lafayette Press, especially to Jessica Hornbuckle who saw the manuscript through to its final stage. And finally, I am most grateful to my wife, Karen, who has been my first reader from the very beginning.

Call and Response: Conversations in Verse (with Jack B. Bedell). Huntsville: Texas Review Press, 2009.
The Blue Boat. Lafayette: The Center for Louisiana Studies, 2004.
Burnt Water Suite. San Antonio: Wings Press, 1999.
The Doors between Us. Hammond: The Louisiana Literature Press, 1997.
Plainsongs. New York: Cross-Cultural Communications Press, 1994.

Versions of some of these poems have appeared in *Alaska Quarterly, Bayou, Connecticut Review, Dallas Review, Die Young, Interdisciplinary Humanities, Louisiana English Journal, Louisiana Literature, Many Mountains Moving, Mid-American Review, Quercus Review, Revista / Review Interamericana, the canary river review, The Louisiana Review, Uncommonplace: An Anthology of Louisiana Poets, Vespers: Contemporary Poems of Religion and Spirituality,* and *Xavier Review.*

In Ordinary Light

New Poems

2004–2009

I

Love is not consolation, it is light.
Simone Weil
Gravity and Grace

And it's ever-present, ev'rywhere.
Van Morrison
"Warm Love"

LIGHT THEOLOGY AND THE PERSIMMON TREE

for Dorothy Bourque Miller

Her kitchen was always filled with ordinary light;
it was the one selected room she made all hers.
From the north window above her sink she gazed
at the white-tailed kites hovering over the ponds,
listened idly to noisy killdeers chattering through
the lazy afternoons in the pasture all summer long.
When she was not satisfied with the lovely things
she could bring us to, she thought selectively about
the fruited hedgerows and orchards this time of year.
Mayhaw jellies and muscadine jams were but some
bright possibilities, but they never passed the test.

Between the *Charadrius vociferus* in the pasture
and that north window was a persimmon tree.
When the skins on the fruit were just beginning
to put on a lemon sheen, she would begin to see
the red-gold they would become. She waited
for the first frost to begin to relax the branches'
hold and for the fruit to go into the manufacture
of the final sugaring before she wrapped each
globe in crisp white tissue. As the year parceled
out its dwindling light, she came to our back doors
before dawn, left us shallow boxes of golden suns.

LUMINA

We're all extensions
        of someone or another's
                golden light.

In the moment
        I was made
                stars filled the sky

& some parts
        of the bodies
                making me

were fleetingly
        illuminated —
                briefly luminous.

Druids see light
        in wood
                and worship trees.

When we wave
        in recognition,
                we disperse light,

set light in motion
        toward
                the beloved.

We string our trees
        with lights
                in wintertime.

We want
        to see ourselves
                in the dark.

THE ANGEL IN MY MOTHER'S BACK

All my sisters and at least one of my aunts think it's angel's wings
growing in my mother's back. She is no longer the baker of breads
she once was, nor the fryer of fishes. She has drifted here to a place
of stillness. She cannot move her legs, cannot even shift her weight

in this bed that has become her tether to this world. On most days
she is all regret framed by the fine silver circle her hair has become,
a halo of sorts if you are schooled in the right iconography. Fazed

by almost nothing in the outside world, she is disconnected from
even her own past it seems, prone, it is true, to grow bone x-rays
tell us. Angel's wings might well be calcified light seeking home

in this world of matter, but my angels work better for me crated
and shipped from little workshops near Carrara, the heavenly face
shaped by human hands working out the math in stone wing-spreads,
by someone who spends time alone, lives in the fulcrum love springs.

THE GYPSY DREAM

after Bill Gingles' *The Gypsy's Dream*

I have put all the parts of this gypsy dream of mine
out on the table. I am weighing what it might say of me
and you. We think sometimes dreams are ragged, fine-
threaded things that seem to ravel and disperse too easily

to mean anything. But try as you might to order everything
and put everything in the right fields and boxes, you will fail
to put the red songs in your head outside your range of singing,

to erase those floating spots dancing somewhere near the pale
skin of your closed eyes. In every dream are interlocking rings
that chain us to who we are, rivers with boats, wind-filled sails

moving us toward ourselves. Our dreams are but one kind
of play we are too tired to play in our waking lives. One tree
we are too weak to climb on the other side is ours to climb
in this other life. The sea you will not swim in, it is your sea.

CÉZANNE'S *BIBEMUS QUARRY*, 1898

It would surprise no one to learn that someone
in Cézanne's family might have been a quilt maker.
He knows the world through geometries
of one kind or another, geometry of sky,
geometry of rock, of trees, of light, water, grass.
His colors he might have taken directly
from *mémere's* wardrobe, the old gray suit
fading to lavender for some rock faces,
the greens from dresses and housecoats
she wore around the house,
the oranges and coppers, her dressy clothes
for those trips to the city.
There were always dark, satiny scraps
from linings for tree trunks
and some pale bunting just right for sky.
What was being done inside houses,
he would do outside for the most part.
He knew the strength of shapes.
He loved the tensile weight of colors.
He wanted more than anything to make a line
hold up whatever was next to it.
He wanted more than anything to let go
as his eye told him to, to hold on
when his hand said *hold on*.
It was his way of covering the world as he saw it.

THE HAND AND THE GOSPEL

In *The Calling of St. Matthew* Caravaggio places
Christ's hand central and just barely below
an open window. That calling hand
is in shadow just below a beam

of bright light. Matthew knows the calling —
of that there is no doubt. His own hand
is visual rhyme with Christ's, and light falling

is full on nearly every face in the little room. Sand
or dirt tracked in by the men in this dawdling
place is carried in the footprints of all but one standing

at the entrance to this room. He has paused, seems
the most contained because he is. This band
of boys and men gambling are stopped, forego
their game. Who it is they are dances on their faces.

THE CALLIGRAPHER'S SON

after Qian Xuan's *Wang Xizhi Watching Geese*

His father could stand for hours watching geese
it seemed to this boy. It was as though
time itself had altered whatever leases
it had on standards set for time. Below

them and nearer the bamboo grove the yellow
water in the pond blazed in sunlight,
set off goose lines, a seeming lighted slough

on which his father made pictograms. Brightness
hammered into lines the old man put in neat rows.
Each mark falling into its proper place, splicing

itself into another line until it ceased
being simply line. Here, a line bowing
like an old tree. Two lines more: cloud eased
onto likeness of rock. There, a hut to grow in.

DES PAPILLONS: WITH OCTA CLARK AND DEWEY BALFA AT MULATES

It is as though these two have found their flower.
The rest of us are moving to their sound,
but they just sit there. This is not high-powered
fare we listen to on other nights but rounds

and jigs and breakdowns and reels. We are sliding
on yellow meal Mulate has sprinkled on the floor,
something to help these heavy feet gliding

but wanting to take to the air at every turn. More
than we could have hoped for, this momentary hiding
inside oblivion. We are taken to another door

where we can see ourselves again. Bridges and towers
are ours to cross and climb. These two do not pound on
anything, their hearts are open windows, ladled hours
in love with all they hear, who they are, what they found.

TUMBLING BLOCKS, AN AMISH QUILT

My great-grandmother was the quilt maker in the family.
    Her mind was not, I think, the kind of mind that could have
        opened to all that controlled disorder in this Amish pattern.

She had everything she needed to manage such configuration,
    and tumbling itself was something she would have understood,
        but not as idea or design. She spent hours at her little machine

next to the light of the east windows on the sun porch, she
    and the machine tucked into baskets of scraps, her rummaging
        through piles of discarded clothes she turned into little squares

filled with surprise. Her color wheel was what she saw in fields
    and her pattern books were stacks of feed sacks that came to her
        from men and boys who worked the fields and fed the cows

and pigs and goats. None of us had trouble sleeping under her quilts.
    Some of us took them with us when we left home to take some notion
        of our places in the world. None of us would have been able to sleep

easily under *tumbling blocks*. We would have had to be too drunk to know
    what covered us or too dog-tired to care. Or stoned on sickness and want.
        But under the wild designs of her versions of tumbling, we slept just fine.

BARDO

after Bill Gingles' *Bardo*

We spend inordinate amounts of time worrying about getting from here
to there. It is a part of our children's games in cars, and we engage them
in part because we too are impatient with this not being in a place where
our minds have settled on as the place we need to be. It is Bethlehem

we want to visit, or Deer Park, or Persepolis, and this wait we're made
to wait is intolerable. What we hardly ever see are the things we carry
with us and how we rhyme them with everything we see. What fades

we meet again with new eyes. Everything we have loved or married
goes with us. The line of demarcation is full and black, lacks shade
of any kind but we never see ourselves walking over it. What varies

between here and there we exaggerate. Whatever it was that was dear
to us in a past life, we throw off all too easily. Something that hemmed
us in there, no worry here in this new place. What was good and fair
we hardly notice. The thick line of boundary is hardly ever the problem.

ISSA

Rain frogs sing their songs
to approaching thunderheads,
Issa, Issa, come.

II

KITCHEN LIGHT

My mother cannot see her kitchen clearly
from where she lies under clean sheets.
It is little more than a narrow hallway now,
a little sink, a little place to drain dishes,
and lots of shelving her eyes never see.
From her bed she hears the microwave,
or the grease popping in the iron skillet
as I pan fry pork chops I've brought her.
She hears the water running or doors
opening and closing, and she sees light
streaming toward her from a shadowy space
her eyes often travel to when I am here.
Years ago it was she who cooked for us.
Years ago she baked bread for the girls
at the school in a neighboring town.
Years ago she feared coming into her house
after dark but she did so anyway.
Years ago she took a certain kind of joy
in the chemistries of making bread,
or at least in the rising and the kneading.
She loved the way the bowls of dough
seemed lighted from within, the way
the enlivened dough took on the sheen
of moons. Rising takes on new meanings
for her these days, as does bread, and dark,
and beds, and whatever it is she cannot see.

THE APPARITION

The old man looking at me through the window
is my father. I wonder how long he's traveled
to get to this place in the yellowing glass. Two
times before he's come to me this way. He unraveled

as quickly as he'd come in those earlier visitations,
but this time he seems a steady bridge between here
and there. I want to walk toward this gauzy temptation,

ask him to dinner, give him cigarettes, offer him a beer,
perhaps take coffee with him at a table — any invitation
or ruse to get him to stay a bit, for once to be near

and not afraid of nearness. But there is no shadow
in this scene. Everything we'd say would be babel.
In this little space there is no above and no below.
One moment in my garden, shade, me raking gravel.

THE BEAM THAT RUNS THROUGH ALL THAT IS HOLY OR MISSHAPEN OR INSPIRED

1

Fools and saints and poets believe
in the upside down,
live under tables where they can escape
the light or create their own.
They name themselves
Luke, or Lucius,
Lucillus or Lucinda.
They can take light pills to sleep
or they might not.
They might love Lucia de Lammermoor
or might never have heard of her.
They illuminate their own worlds mostly.
Light is forever drawing away or
coming at them. Light is lucre,
luck or lack of it, hermitage,
desert, prayer, homage,
the pilgrimage to the inside,
the journey outside.

2

Light is the equalizer.
The saint feels it.
As did Dürer and Hopper,
Caravaggio and Rembrandt.
Painters migrate south
for the right light.
Bellini made shafts lighted.
Photographs, light paintings.
Shakespeare wrote light sonnets.
Jerome had desert light.
Luke has gospel light.
Speilberg knows ET light.
Scorcese speaks light language.
Cocteau split his love
between beast light
and beauty light.
Gypsies sit by fires
all their lives
then burn their wagons
when they die.
Pirates open light chests.
Hitler died in darkness.
One dark afternoon, Christ died.
Buddha sat in shade and darkness.
He waited for light.
It came.
Wordsworth breathed light.
Whitman followed light.
Dickinson and Vermeer,
Matisse and de Hooch,
and Bonnard too,
all loved windows.

THE ANGEL OF DESIRE

first line from Mary Oliver's "Reckless Poem"

Sometimes already my heart is a red parrot, perched
on the window sill overlooking the garden
filled with gingers this time of year. Like
gingers it repeats itself all over the place

"I want, I want, I want," it says to anyone
who will listen. It wants to leave heart print
everywhere. It cares neither more for sun

or shade; it looks for place to roost. Flinty
stone ledge or goose-down bed — it's all one
and the same to this demented knot. Twenty

times, the same as one. Tracery leads to trace,
trace to path, path to major thoroughfare. Kites
and eagles both fly. Herons, crows and martins —
inflected recall. Habitual heart, airy bobbin, parched.

MY FATHER AT BAT

My father is batting balls to me
in the pasture. My hands are small
and my glove keeps opening
like a flat pan, my fingers barely
reaching into the glove's fingers.
The morning rain has gathered
into little puddles he tells me
I must not even be aware of
if I am to ever get good at this
thing he is teaching me.
He says the glove must become
a second skin. He pops a fly
and for an instant it is the blue
cloudlessness that catches my eye.
I am thinking I must be a holy mess
to him. He just keeps batting
ball after ball after ball.
At school all this ends
with a bell eventually ringing.
Here, there are no bells to save me.
It's just me and him.
He is strong.
He is doing what he has to do.
And the sun is still high in the sky.

EZRA POUND IN PISA

> *It troubles my sleep.*
> —"Cantico del Sole" in *Instigations*

When they caged him in the piazza
he found himself
transformed
somewhat.
He could have been any one
of those people who take wrong
turns and end up badly.
A reporter in search of a story
might have asked if he knew
the works of Rilke or of Kafka,
and if they spoke to him.
Whether he growled incoherent
obscenities or not, we don't know.
A man wearing a tuxedo
came up to the cage.
The old poet could have screamed
Don't leave until you've finished
but he didn't.
When someone finally came
with a ring of keys
I can hear him muttering
it troubles my sleep,
when they pulled him out
of the cage
it troubles my sleep,
when they shipped him home
it troubles my sleep,
when they tied him to his bed
in St. Elizabeth's
it troubles my sleep,
when they released him
to his friends
it troubles my sleep

when he lived on and on
it troubles my sleep,
when in Venice in solitude
it troubles my sleep.

LINCOLN IN NEW ORLEANS, 1831

When he arrived that year he had to walk
a mile or so on flatboats to reach the shore.
He had poled and floated here, watched hawks
circling overhead on lazy afternoons, still bore

the scar he'd gotten years before when he chased
and fought off seven fugitive slaves who tried to rob him
and his measly crew near Baton Rouge. He pasted

some home remedy on the gash and then stemmed
the blood with some cloth he had on board. It lasted
all his life, this scar over his right eye but it hemmed

in nothing. What really lasted was the chatter and talk
around Maspero's Exchange where one mulatto girl more
was trotted and pinched, undressed while buyers gawked
and ciphered for the lowest price they could get her for.

SAKYONG MIPHAM AT THE NEW YORK CITY MARATHON

Just when you begin to think Buddhists don't run,
running past you near Central Park at Trump's place
is Sakyong Mipham Rinpoche, no way to tell him
from the other runners. Here he is as ordinary as air.

Just when you begin to think you know the nun
and what it is she is supposed to do, she races
through expectations of nuns. This slim
girl can see her work, see herself already there.

They will rebuild the college facing the Great Eastern Sun.
They see themselves in water perhaps, two of many faces
readying themselves to occupy their bodies, trim
themselves to the ins and outs of mind and body paired.

Just when you begin to think Shambhala is lost in airy depth,
you are just breathing and there it is dissolving on your breath.

AVE MARIA: ANOTHER QUEENLY VERSION

If she could have told it, it would be a different story altogether
than the ones we are used to hearing. In the stories not hers
she is dressed in the flowing robes queens on this earth wear.
She is crowned with precious metal crowns with jewels in them;

she walks on moons, crushes snakes, and stars encircle her head
as though she is some interplanetary goddess. She even floats
on clouds, and in one version she is a pagan goddess who's shed

all her clothes to rise from murky seas and drift toward waiting oats,
toward flowers and fruit trees. She is offered a mantle rich and red,
a silken embroidered fullness to cover nakedness in a land of goats.

But, she may have dreamed nothing. A quiet fish in her belly swam.
She connected to nothing; she, a sheet night can be, no oaths or swears
inside it. She made way for a thing erasing her, no sighs, no verse
to interrupt a thing — indecipherable, undelineated, inexplicable forever.

HIDDEN HILLS: FINAL LESSONS

We were sitting near the lake in fading light, a place
particularly his. He had just put on his feeding tube,
his walk deliberate, his voice still ragged and frail
from the team of surgeons's recent work on him.

I had expected to see some ravage, perhaps a face
gaunt and pulled, but here he was spilling rubrics
for making poems. Words loved crawl like snails,
he said, then lift. Flight, or something near, new skin,

configured miracles. Words, like organs, pace
themselves into surge and flow, beat like rude
and lusty hearts to new geographies. Unafraid of jail
sentences or other tedious punishments put on them,

they rattle bars and refuse to sit. They sing in their cells,
teach prose a new tango move or two, even temper hells.

THE UNMARKED GRAVE

for Jacques Thibodeaux

It may have everything to do with not being able to find you.
As a kid I watched you watching us over my great-grandmother's bed
and by the time I was old enough to ask, you had faded into some blue
memory she did not even want to talk about. Or could not. Instead

she'd dismiss you with some quip stammered
out as though you were nothing to her. But still
she kept the image of you. When one nail rusted, she hammered

in another to keep you with us. The chill
in the fall air as I look for you is sharp. The clamor
in the graveyard among the white-washers and grass-cutters is stilled

occasionally by something or another time has turned to quiet duty.
I take out my yellowed map from the rectory, the one I've read
a thousand times it seems and still there are no leads, no clue
to where you lie, no blaze of name, no proximity to anything among the dead.

BASHO

Pecan trees open
green parasols on green fields —
this year's work half done.

IN ORDINARY LIGHT

after *The Little Street (1658)*
Johannes Vermeer, 1632–1675

Under the green shutters two children play —
a game of jacks perhaps or perhaps they are intent
on progress of ants or other bugs. It is but one day
where doing what you need to with ease seems sent

finally. Everyone is unhurried and unremarkable here.
Yet, there is the crescent of a moon on the shoulder
of the woman who may be drawing clear
water from a barrel, sly slivered rhyme for the bolder

half-moon on the half-painted portal above her.
The woman hunched over sewing wears a red shirt
beneath a yellow blouse and over that a white cover
of some kind. A miracle the way all the white skirting

in the painting offsets the weight of the upper stories —
perturbed Dutch clouds and red rhymes, other glories.

VIEW OF THE SUNSET AT MEGURO

from *View of the Sunset at Meguro*
Ando Hiroshige, 1797–1858

Autumn maples are foregrounded in this view of the sunset at Meguro.
Hiroshige has stilled nearly everything. Here there are no bridges
to other places. Bridges must be beyond the yellow hills or below
the dark blue waters in the part of the stream we see. Near the ridge

we know people live in little huts, diminutive, stacked echoes
of the vast rising, the holding luminescence far in the distance.
The farmers here are rice farmers. Look at the singular hoe

on one of the farmer's shoulders near the tree. What chance
makes him walk away from the other workers walking slowly,
going home? Does he have more work to do, or are his pants

rolled because he's now paid a debt and has to cross this low
rice land to his own village? The leaves are falling, the sedge
is thinning in the shallow waters near him. Light does not grow
on any surface. He and everything around him tend a darkening edge.

WINTER LIGHT

for Sandy Lyne

It is the winter sky I fall in love with again this year.
It can be heavy bearing, this unrelieved gravity, flat gray
broad board of sky that covers nearly everything. But
surely it is precisely that very blankness it is which calls

us to its indefinite perimeters. It is that gray, drear
insistence that gives this sky its other miracles: days
opening, the orange lamp of the eastern edges cut
by some impatient child-god for his stage set. All

that colored light flooding onto surfaces, clearing
and cleaning everything it falls upon: roans and bays
in the fields breathing their frosty breaths, the mutts
following their mother in the tall grasses, water falling

like crystal from the eaves. Then gray's recession into night,
a blue sparkled heaven, chimeras, archers, or almost no light.

THE TRANSCENDENCE ANGEL

Form is emptiness; emptiness is form.
— The Heart Sutra

How can I know how much of you is in me
unless I tilt the bowl and let you go?
How can I measure memory unless I spread it out
on a page, see its volume with my own eyes,
feel its weight in my own hands?
The things I cannot say
I cannot bring before me.
I cannot see the curve of anything
unless I see the curve of things outside me.
When I empty heaven
from what I know of heaven,
heaven has new fields to grow in.
When I empty myself of myself,
I lose what I have carried around
with me all these years.
I am new and nothing, a sacred text of emptiness.

THE DUCKS AT LAKE DES ALLEMANDS

for Marcia Gaudet

The lake at Des Allemands is a strong brown plate
under a cowl of trees. In autumn and winter
trunks hold bold and sure calligraphy. In late
spring sedges push through the edge's splintered

light. Duckweed laces the water near the banks
where Muscovy and mallards paddle through
a daytime moon just barely floating there. Flanks

of irises wait to receive the waves a separated few
make in their play amounting to what might rank
as almost nothing in grander schemes of things. Two

kinds of ducks, a lake, sedge, duckweed ruff, we take
this kind of beauty in stride. But in such rough plenty
abides both loss and dark, latent reminders of our fate.
Initial loss of imperceptibles, then everything uncentered.

AT DUSK AS WE PREPARE FOR THE LEONIDS

The pond in the far pasture turns yellow
in this dwindling light, becomes the light
itself as everything slips quietly off. Mallows
lose their pink and red this time of day. Kites

have flown off to wherever it is kites fly
to when night falls, and whatever it is the day
has hammered out is flattened. Whatever cry

pierced and blazed is mute — cicadas, cardinals, jays
have all gone quiet for the evening birds. A sigh
so faint we think it is the ghost of sound stays

the ghost of sound in trees. Whatever falls in light has fallen
and whatever it is that brightens in darkness slowly brightens.
Someone seeing us from a distance might think this a fallow
time, but in hours heavy metal will look like stars in flight.

GARDENS

Men milk goats and mares in Darius' garden.

Kunitz's snakes hang from a tree. He watches from
a distance & makes a poem for the breathless moment.

Prayer wheels turn in gardens in Tibet.

Nuns move quietly among the chrysanthemums
in the gardens in Kyoto. Some pull grass. Some hum.

Crickets can't tell the garden from heaven.

Water falling from the eaves in Kaplan. The tin drum
was just a shallow basin before the rains came.

Monet never feared wild growth.

Buddha sits at the base of a tree in his garden
& Jacob's trellis is forever filled with climbing angels.

At Sissinghurst white shades filled Vita's garden.

In my garden tomatoes teach lessons in silence
& dissertations on sweetness are written in honeycombs.

In Christ's garden he knelt and fought despair.

Chagall talked to Moses in his garden, of Canaan
they could go to now, of light they could live in.

WHEN IT RAINS

It could have been in one of those waiting stations
near the falls in some mountain pass in China.
The candy wrapper said *Buy Yourself Flowers,* a fortune
of sorts. The last time it happened it was a bird
we thought might have been the Holy Ghost hovering
over her just out of reach. She said it was not.
For over a week now my wife's mother has been trying
to talk to us about blue roses. The Veilchenblau
we ordered should arrive in mid-January along with
Formosa azaleas we are putting in near the bamboo
hedge. I learned today that yellow dock is *la patience,*
that some Natives call the dandelion *pissenlit.*
My friend Barry tells me the old people called the path
the cows make in the pastures *une routine.*
I have taken to looking for the crows every morning
on my run, the way they set my path right again.
They seem to be laughing often at the dark reflection
they fly above with ease. *Just us,* they belt out. Then,
Not afraid, right over the shade they make. *Just us.*
The Chinese fall in love with ancient trees, will crook
a road to save one. The Japanese love raked gravel
and boulders in their gardens, and mosses and willows.
They love flower petals and red leaves in still and slow-
moving waters, love chartreuse maples and hollyhocks.
The Japanese and the Chinese love many of the same things
but they don't say so often. They are often reserved, reticent
about such loose talk. The damask in the drapes
in the hotel comes from a rose in Syria, perhaps
a sport from a bush in some walled garden in Teheran.
Li Po may have drunk his rice wine near reflecting pools,
or dreaming of falls in the mountains he would travel to,
or walking through the citrus groves. Wine, poem, rain.
The way water falls off a corrugated tin roof, the way
it brings gravel up, ridge of tiny pebbles, little volcanoes
under clear water with clear water falling into them.

KISSING IN KOSOVO, 1999

A mother may be talking about the years
it usually takes to get back to a place
once you have been away for a while. Bells
will always ring at their appointed times
above villages everywhere, and somewhere
someone will be separated from nearly all
engagements except kissing, inordinately
long kissing, what all this day has been
tending toward all day long. The schools
are telling their children their jobs
and their lives depend on learning tables
of one sort or another and the children
are learning the geometry and the calculus
of kissing. Men and women are kissing
each other in bed, behind trees, in lakes,
at the seashore.   A boy pulls a girl to him.
He is still straddling his bicycle. He
is kissing hard and slow between classes.
Men will want to be kissing all the time.
Women will too. Both wonder when the kiss
will come right finally. Roofs will go on
being orange, or ochre, or red. Roofs will
glisten after the rain. Roofs will brighten
when the sun comes out before the wet has
finally lifted. Someone will be kissing
beneath the orange or ochre or red roofs.
Women will continue to wash their hair
at the well where other women are gathering
water for beans or bread, or soup for those
who will want to kiss after they have eaten.
Women will continue to wash their hair in
sinks, tubs, buckets, showers. One woman
lifts her head, wraps her hair in a towel,
large, thirsty, white. She sees her image
in the glass before her. She is in love
momentarily with what she sees. Kisses her-

self lightly as she slides away. Old men
are grabbing boys by the scruff of the neck.
Old women will pull boys around by the ears
like they were goats. This is what they do
when they can't get a sufficiency of kissing
into their lives. Streets will be chalky
white as they always were, or black as mud.
On them will be people going to places
where they hope they will be delivered
finally to a plenitude of kissing. Lemons
sweeter than you thought lemons could be
will lie half-peeled in bowls on tables.
The peelers are dreaming kissing.
A boy will ask about his father who went
to war. The answer he gets will not be
enough for him. He thinks he is beginning
to forget his father. He will kiss the image
fading in his head. He will not wipe it away.

RECEIPTS & OTHER DOCUMENTATION

It turns out I was there after all.
When my wife asks on what day I mailed the bills
or picked up the laundry, or at what time
the UPS man delivered the package,
I haven't a clue. It is clear to me though
that these things have been done &
that there is evidence to be uncovered
if there were ever such a need to show
exactly when the brown truck with yellow
lettering rolled into our part of the world.
There is evidence, for sure, to know exactly
when the Blaze roses were delivered
& on exactly what day last fall we drove
to St. Francisville to visit friends and eat
at the Magnolia Café. Who or what
hammered this retrieval system
out of my brain is as much a mystery to me
as the unretrievable details themselves.
I take comfort in the fact that much of this part
of the story is recorded by someone, somewhere,
and that I was there after all.

HERON, IRIS, RAIN

There is a kind of ordinary miracle
that might set us up for bigger ones
to come. *Drala* when it shows itself
as such in Tibet, or in any other home,

is just that kind of thing. Everything
falls away from what is commonplace;
much outside your ordinary eye swims

away toward some other pull, a string
of cattle egrets rising from some fascial
rest rise toward a notion of miracle twin

unseen. It can be that way with bells,
unscaled fish, ports and dutiful drones
even. Anything almost can turn itself —
heron, iris, rain— you inside this poem.

TOBIAS, A FISH, AN ANGEL

Tobias had fished often as a boy. Fish turning
into heavenly things he had never seen before.
His fish drifted usually; big lazy configurations,
shadows in murky light. If on rare days he found

them in clearer pools, it was motion's dazzled
luminaries he caught darting in and out of glass,
fractious rainbows he placed in the tall grasses

to keep them cool. He could hardly be misled
in these things he knew so well. But the grasps
this one held him to was something new. Crisis

he could hardly understand — this new ground,
this shaky alliance underfoot, new ministrations
to consider. Far from home he listened to more
than he fathomed: angel, fish, the eye of morning.

BUSON

We know this garden.
The riverbank at Kema
will soon be in sight.

From *Plainsongs*

1994

ELMIRE

pour ma grand grand-mère
Elmire David Thibodeaux (1875–1969)
et son mari, Jacques

Je me demande
combien de temps
t'as espéré

ou si tu
savais même
qu'il s'était échappé

de toi et de ton
ventre gonflé

long temps avant le point de jour
pour arranger une barrière

dans la gelée
de février.

Le vieux portrait
sur le mur nous dit
tout ce qu'on connaît

de sa jeunesse
de sa force
et de ses traits simples.

On veut faire quelque chose
de ce petit bon esprit
au dessus de ton lit.

To ajoutes seulement
quand on te demande
que t'avais seize ans

que tu te rappelles pas
d'un tas. Il a été dehors
pour arranger un barrière
et il est mort.

ELMIRE

for my great-grandmother
Elmire David Thibodeaux (1875–1969)
and her husband, Jacques

I wonder
how long
you waited

or if you
even knew
he had slipped

from you and your
six-months bulging belly

long before daybreak
to mend a fence

in the February
frost.

The old picture
on the wall tells
us all we know

of his youth
and strength
and clean features.

We want to make something
of this handsome boy-
ghost over your bed.

You only add
when we ask
that you were sixteen,

that you don't remember
much. He went out
to fix a fence
and died.

NATIVE GROWTH

In some parts cypress and men are called *azad*. Free.
They bear no fruit, have nothing to give away.
The tree is ever-flourishing, the man at one with God.
But here our pale green, feathered tree turns,
loses its leaves, bears cones. The wood everlasting
begins in perfect pyramid, then grows scraggled
and gnarled; it reaches not only up but out.
It is of the seasons. Like an old man who knows the way
but keeps losing his direction, it stands with open spaces.

EGRETS AT BEAN CUTTING TIME

Unlike their finer cousins whose plumes
were sought to set off epaulets
or nestle in some artful head,
these plain birds rise noisily in full billow
from the bean fields bare and brown. Like fine
Belgian lace beating in from the window's
golden autumn air, they fly together long
enough to approximate pattern. Then break.
Here swirling. There cutting back and down
again. And farther on, straight ahead,
those not knowing or not caring for movement,
or pattern, or even for flying alone. Over
these fields my bird self meets his kin,
sometimes leaving, sometimes wheeling.
Then falling. Finally falling earthward.
A paraclete rain against the color of coins.
Ancient. Newly uncovered. Smelling sweet.

PLAINSONGS OF THE *MARAIS BOULEUR*

1

On most days my thoughts
run straight and green,
flat and unbroken as the fields.

The water moccasin and the skunk,
opossum and mink, nutria and racoon
run in straight rows patched
to the horizon on every side.

My cajun squeeze box
plays no sharps nor flats.
All is ground level.

2

Above the southwest prairie
the blue is filled with mountains
of cloud —

indigo, black, violet, white,
some pink, some like heaps
of flaked salmon on large blue plates,
but most lapping, rising, boiling

while the afternoon rattles
like the troubadours of old Provence,
beating at the gate,
ready for the show.

3

Listen to their names.

What they call themselves.
Amar
Amos
Amat
Aristile
Albertine
Angelas
Odile
Odon
Claudia
Elise
Jean-Baptiste
Jacques
Theodule
Valerie
Nana
Asa
Zoa
Fernest
Elmire
Philoman

4

Pairs of shoes lined up
just inside the back door,
or sometimes on the back steps.
The dirt or dust or mud
we've picked up along the way
left near the threshold.

5

My mother and my aunts
are the girls who scrub
the floors with lye.

The planks dry white,
like syrup candy
they pull on winter nights.

6

In November black lines move
across a colorless sky, calling.
A man, wherever he is, looks up.
A woman comes out of the house
and off the porch. She looks up.
A child stops, looks up, points.
They shift, positioning themselves
for the planting of winter's sound.

THE EASTER MEAL

This is not something we do in courses.
Sometimes after the adults *pacque* eggs
and the children hunt for them,
everything is brought to the table
at one time.

After the fresh ham, the turkey, and pork roast,
all scored and glazed, pierced and stuffed
with dry cayenne peppers and minced garlic,
after the oyster dressing, the creamed spinach,
after the salad of chopped broccoli,
zucchini and yellow squash, water chestnuts,
slivered almonds and pine nuts,
romaine and red-leafed lettuce.
After the crab and crawfish and shrimp-
stuffed *mirlitons*. After all this
and the chocolate rabbit cake with raspberry sauce,
the table levitates.

The silver dulls on the dark blue cloth.
The island in the dining room drifts
into the rest of the house.
We go to our posts like the tired sailors
we are, look out at seas we know will swim on
again, or sail in again to find our way home.
But not for now, this charting
or this uncovering of strategies
for a return that will get most of us home.
Not now.
Some of us do not even want to go home.

For now, just the gazing, glaze-eyed,
turkey and pig fat turning to lotus blossoms
in our bellies,
and the forgetting,
ah, the forgetting.

BURNING THE CHAFF

As children we often wondered
if that afternoon near the combine

something like the air's heat hit within

or hurled itself from outside
straight into Mr. Dolph's brain.

The workmen near him in the field

that day say they feared
his thrashing might throw an arm

or more into the blades. He did

not just fall. It was as if he
saw it coming, took the terror

with him as he fought. Let go

only when he had to.
What he could never have planned on

were the years fixed

in sheets, stiff, clean,
perfumed. With only two words

left in him. *Goddamn.*

Positive.
Each afternoon the sun crossing

the room to lie on him.

His broad-hipped wife scraping
calloused feet across worn linoleum

bringing him soup and this life.

LE COURIR DE MARDI GRAS

De bonne heure le matin, tous les hommes
du grande courir se mettent en ligne
derrière notre capitaine, tout habillé
en rouge de passion. En cône et en cape
ressemblant à des malfaiteurs perdus d'un autre temps,
il nous mène d'un bord à l'autre de la campagne,
àyou on descend à toutes les maisons,
levant des nuages de poussière.
Après battre le temps de la mélodie.
Le petit fer sonne e l'accordéon braille.
Des fois, méme de bonne heure don la journée,
on prend nos frères dans les bras et on chante
et on danse, obliant qu'on est masqués.
On est pris dans l'acte. On est
le feu et l'air. On va pas se rappeler
avant demain, notre séparation
et qu'on est aussi la terre.

LE COURIR DE MARDI GRAS

Early in the morning all the men
of the *grande courir* line up
behind our leader, dressed in passion's
red. In cone and cape, looking like
a lost marauder of another time,
he takes us through the countryside
where we dismount at every house,
raising clouds of dust. Beating out
the tune. It is all triangle ring
and squeeze box strain. Sometimes,
even early in the day, we take our
brothers in our arms as we sing and
dance, forgetting we wear masks.
We get caught up in the act. We are
fire and air. We will not remember
until tomorrow our separateness,
and that we are also earth.

GARDEN SPIDERS AND SUMMER RAINS

Spanning poles and trees, power lines and summers,
the *argiope aurantia* return to do their work.
They insure for another year my part in the tale
about the man who grows spiders at his house;
keep the mosquito hordes in check; always ready
when thunderheads come across the southwest prairie
to hang head-down in the rain, the six front legs
loose, the two back ones clipped on their webs —
swinging like heavy jewels from gypsies' ears.

THE CONSECRATION OF EARS AND TONGUES

1

The late afternoon sky holds it shape
at the end of summer in the *marais*,
like some abstractionist had taken to it,
tricking us momentarily.
Before the light behind it finally goes,
broad gray-black strokes rub
barely perceptible tremolos
on a color field with just a touch
of amber in it. This new dark sky, not sky
at all until the eye catches Venus
in the west, and one or two attendant stars
restore the firmament to its name.
There is no story here. No chronology
to get us from here to there.
In this sky there is no sound,
or none as we usually think of sound.
But I am listening, ear pressed against
the air, for someone like Mahler perhaps,
and for what he may have made of such
a sky. How he would have not just punctuated
the silence but made it sound, how he would
have pierced streaks with counterpoint
stretching the whole expanse:
sky in the cello's lower registers
pulling itself from itself.
Here and there he would perhaps
have marked the dark strokes with folk tune,
here and there with clash of steel
on steel. Now and again you would hear
strings pushing higher and higher,
an ascension where we hold on
to see if we can hear when he pushes
finally beyond sound, we thinking
perhaps we still hear the high whine

in the silence he holds until we know
that whatever it is we are hearing
we have brought to the score.
And just before we might intrude,
he repeats the cello's phrase, this time
two octaves lower, again sustaining
sound until we begin to suspect
we are hearing all this time
some inquiry. Huge, elaborate variations
of sound not usually perceived as sound.

2

Father, you, in love with silences,
even you would have begged relief.
In this last light of day, I hear
the cold and the dark of mornings
I drove you to work. So in love
with silences, you rarely broke it
with your own voice,
                    as though you
had only so much sound to use, and
only so much of that to make words
with, so you guarded your allotment
as if it were cut out of God's silence,
given especially to you, him
testing you, counting on you
to love the word, sacramentalize it,
love the work given to you, never
to profane it, always to figure
how to spend what was given
and where.
                    Even you
would hear in the falling pitch
of those dark caves where sound is
always breathing its last breath,
a betrayal, or something close to it,

something left out of the original
negotiation, some gift we cannot leave
unattended, this gift the first covenant,
not housed completely in hand or throat
but in dialogue between lobes
on either side of some central fissure
in the forebrain. Not completely inside
ourselves or outside where the eye rests.
Something larger perhaps than whispering
over cerebrum faults in our own heads.
Whatever passes is a rover passing through,
               passing through
us and through what we call world, weaving
it to us and us to it, now through eyes,
now through tongues, now through hands,
as if sound itself is a lover reaching
for the soft meat just above your hips,
a prelude to the small death awaiting you
in a room where if do you hear sound,
it will be sound you have never heard before
like that, a place of no light
you have ever called light before.
This quintessential loiterer not noticed
at all in port or square or roaming
through the countryside
               or barely noticed
by those assuming net mending or some other
ordinary task was the work at hand.
In those dark near absences of sound
I was about to say, you were, father,
something on the verge of sound
on those cold mornings at the wheel
leaning into phosphorescent green light
looking for voices other than your own
to break the silence.
               Voices
we both loved because they did their work,
because they were flatter than the prairie

we lived in, voices singing of rings
of fire and fallen angels, voices singing
of cold hearts and cheating hearts,
voices contracted with silence,
the words holding for some short time
here, some surge almost of articulation
of something before they blur and become
just sound once again.

3

Today I listen to music without words,
the kind the sky in the *marais* makes.
Father, I am making a song
of first sounds to hold us until
the language of words works again.
Father, I, too, am leaning into waves
of sound and light. Whatever they will give,
I am placing on tongues and ears
like holy bread or burning coal. Here,
we will make ourselves out of whatever
sound comes to us. Here, where
it is never clear if consecration
is in the act of choosing or if
the possibility of choice before the act
itself is consecration. Here, where
as in most great loves, it is never clear
who the chooser is and who the chosen.

THE BODY AS BABEL

O holy mystery. O Babylon. O gate of God,
my body. Begin anywhere and I am at a loss
to understand. You want to begin with heart,
blue and rubbery cells that call me to something
as ungrammatical as love? Love of a woman,
love of man, love of generations locked in stone
in mountains, love of generations just beginning
their move through deserts so they can become
hearts too. The stranger in my breast, the stranger
in yours, beating a tongue against our throats.
How close can we get to that song the heart sings?
How to be one with the drifter the human heart is?
But don't stop there. Try spleen. Or kidney.
Or pancreas. Try landing on the islands
of Langerhans, try charting a course
to the interstitial tissues, the small places
between things that govern how much sweetness
your blood can carry. Try brain. Or try
that small pink fish I've been walking behind
all my life. Begin with the walk to communion
rails with that one stretched out like some salmon
leaping rapids and falls in a blind and fatal run
home. Try reading Nietzsche when that one would
rather swim. Try being unremoved with this speaker
of tongues in your lap. Try being in place
with that one if you can. Or try praying
a prayer in a language you have not learned yet.
O holy mystery. O Babylon. O gate of God,
my body.

LOVE AMONG TREES AND FISHES

It is hard to keep things apart here.
The warm wet air rising from warm,
wet earth is palpable.
If we didn't breath this air everyday,
we'd feel its wetness in nostrils
and lungs. If we didn't see the world
everyday, we might think our cayenne fields
were fish ponds, all those small red fish up
for the feeding in that green sea in green air.
Irises floating in our yards swim there
like blue Orana and Ryukan carp.
And mallows everywhere: okra for gumbos,
musk mallow and marsh mallow in ditches
and low ground, cotton on high ground,
Roses of Sharon and Stars over Jerusalem
in our gardens. Our large trees sprout ferns
on branches, sprout true mosses in crooks
& crevices. Other mosses lose their roots
to hang in our trees like silver fish.
Here they are lovers reaching and swaying
for what is dark and beyond them always.
For this air they would leave everything
behind. They would give everything
to the branches over them or the branches
under them. They would even swim again
in smaller, noisier sleeps they've come from
for this turning and drifting, the whole body
feeding on ripe air without ever fully waking.

FEEDING THE OPOSSUM

To come to us he must cross
a stretch of open lawn.
He lives in a field near our house
in Johnson grass and golden rod,
in pecan, walnut and pine,
in thistle and tea weed,
in mimosa and magnolia and cottonwood
seeded by bird and beast and wind.
He lives there in that field
and beyond.
To come to us he must cross
one board fence, a stretch of concrete.
He does not know pools.
If he steps into the sky
we have brought to the ground
to cool us when we might break into flame,
I will fish him out.
I will remember nearly every time
I do so a part of him lives
in one of my daughters
who saw only his tail one day
in a dark corner when she was five
and flew through the door of the wash house,
the blood gone from her face, *a snake
with hair,* she reported, terror
and joy drumming from miles
or ages deep in her. The devout
make *awful* into a word for that dark brilliance
she felt in that hour.
The anthropologist is *awed* as in his bone
he sees farther into the light
at both ends of his cave. I will see
nearly every time I pull him from the water
a bloated stomach and a fuzzy face
that is me living outside the fence
and beyond. To come to us

71

he must cross lawn and concrete
and water obstacle and yet another
board fence. But he comes
to the tin filled with food
for cats. And I walk to the back door
at night, switch on the outside light
to see if he is there. He comes
mostly in the dark or in the daytime
when he senses we are in the house
busy with dusting or washing dishes,
or when I am at a place deep
in my own darkness, digging
& sifting for a light of my own, shaping words
as I would shape bread, portioning pieces
of grain, earth, iron, air, fire, and water
into tins and placing them in ovens.
The clicks of his paws on the bricks
are rhymes for the clicks of the machine
I sit before, rhymes for the clicks
in the metal as the oven heats and cools.
If I get lost and must walk around awhile
to find myself, I go to the back door
on the pretense of checking to see
if the sky is still blue or if Venus
is where I left her last.
I open the door sometimes, walk past him
or closer to him. I know I will pull him
from his table of sorts. I tell myself
I am checking to see if this fall
iron will burn in the pyracantha berry
along the second board fence from the house.
I must do this over and over again
day and night. He will crawl
into the crotons against the bath house wall
and I will go to the fire thorn.
He will move into the four o'clocks
or euonymus or any semblance or cluster
resembling where he lives. Or we both

will go just beyond the first fence
and wait. He, at least in part,
for easy food. I, for myself,
for the daughter who must be fed
in the memory, for the bloated belly
and fuzzy face I see in mirrors
and windows of reflecting glass, I
for myself, against hunger,
feeding myself and climbing
into the fire of crotons and out again.

COUNTRY NIGHTS

Every night we gathered
      on the porch for nightly check.
Like clerks at inventory time

      we reported the losses;
what was missing,
      what had been spent,

or stolen, we thought,
      and what was needed
as we drifted into pauses.

      Again each evening we learned
to wait as we were waiting
      and would surely wait again,

for the black itself to form
      patterns beyond light,
beyond sound,

      beyond loneliness.
Then we moved
      into the house for the night

carrying inside us
      designs of the spaces
between stars.

SUMMER LIGHT IN EARLY AFTERNOON

Here in my yard the sun turns the morning green.
Grass, the green of grasses everywhere laid upon
with gentle light. Trees take on this probing too,
this penetration, like lovers. This stuff shot into
and through their cells, they are not tree, nor grass,
nor bush without. Azaleas sing pink and purple,
peach and salmon praises in return. New bananas
and gingers, each blade, chanteuse, each one
the only one who could know her lavender heart
paling in her breast each second she is not singing
in her circle of light. The high, clear yellows
in the jasmine on the back fence, in lemon lilies
circling the drive, lift soprano voices against all
that blue rubbing closer to the ground. Stubborn-
seeming ones even, their names thrust out before
them like taunting capes — camellia, ligustrum,
oak — their names a false bravura, their seeming
opacity but thin machismo. They, too, open
lusty, hungry mouths, take the fiery tongues deep
into their hearts simply because they cannot live
without them there. They could no more answer
why they are not translucent green lamps turned on
and left to burn in the morning air by someone
walking through the house than we could
when later in the day everything goes, not white
exactly, but colorless or color transcended,
and we are asked what color grass is. Green
we would say without faltering. Green, of course,
we would say, as grass is everywhere, thinking
the asker strange perhaps, but not more strange
than the world we live in is strange. This world
always recognizable, if recognition is a requisite
witness & witness is what is called for in light
so fierce, but really, not so recognizable at all.

FISH WITH GLASSES

My oldest daughter's first drawing,
a fish with glasses. It slips into a white sea
under her hands.

When we see it, it swims head on
past the undercolor of white on white. Blood
red, it waves

its exaggerated fins. It holds itself
in both the first and last water it will swim in. The same
color as the fish,

this water closest to us, a network
of horizontal lines clearly put on last. They waver so,
it is difficult to tell

how many there are. They mark some river
or some sea the fish will go to. Some water boundary
stopping it. Or something

holding it. The near-sighted fish
is happy, its fins shifting as it slow dances,
wide-eyed, between there and here.

FOR A SUMMER MORNING AND FOR THE THINGS THEMSELVES

Centuries ago Amarantha lets down her hair.
Rachel puts together one of Mozart's pieces
this morning and dust dances in shafts of light.

The figs I've taken from the icebox
glaze themselves on the kitchen table.
On the sun porch, Easter thirty years ago,

my uncles play *bourrée* in starched white shirts
and drink whiskeys in spit-shined shoes.
Today the air takes on no adjectives. Sound

stays sound. Dust is only dust. Uncles
and figs would have it another way but remain,
for a while at least, just figs and uncles.

HAECCEITAS

Je suis après marcher
les chemins dans
cette sainte prairie.
Je suis après dormir
dans les fossés.
Mes yeux
sant après diviser
le monde en
quartre morceaux,
puis dans toutes
les directions
entre eux.
Mes oreilles
sont après entendre
la musique que
je jongle est
pas là
quand je jongle que
le vent a parti, quelque part d'autre.
Je suis après faire des cahiers
des herbes dans les prairie.
Je suis après faire des chansons
avec les noms de arbres.
Je suis couché
sur cette terre sante
pour rencontrer
les intelligences
dans ces chambres,
pour connaître
quelle cellules
disent
ou comment les cellules
disent —
asteur glissez,
asteur volez, asteur
tournez.

HAECCEITAS

I am walking
the paths in
this holy plain.
I am sleeping
in its ditches.
My eyes
are dividing
the world in
four pieces,
then in all
the directions
in between.
My ears
are hearing
music I think
is not there
when I think
the wind has
gone elsewhere.
I am making notebooks
of the grasses
in the prairie.
I am making songs
with the names
of trees.
I am lying down
on this holy
ground to meet
the intelligences
in these rooms,
to know
what cells
say
or how cells
say —
now slither,

now fly, now
turn.

From *The Doors Between Us*

1997

&

From *Burnt Water Suite*

1999

THE GRAMMAR OF VERBENAS

I am turning from my mother. I am moving
to the person with the camera perhaps,
a single verbena blossom in my right hand.
The date on the Fox snapshot tells me now
I am six. I am turning or being turned
by it, a flame I am holding to someone
higher, a flame I am ready to offer
to someone bigger than I am. Others
are in the shot, two sisters, an aunt,
little more than a child herself
looking off into the distance. Granny,
my great-grandmother, always turned
her face to the side when she knew
her image was being made. She was there.
Looking off into another distance,
her nose almost touching her chin.
We used to say when she took out her teeth
she could have brought them together
if she could have been persuaded to try.
But I don't think it was any of these
people in the picture.
                    I think it was
someone outside the field who said something
that put weight and form into the flower.
It was like that moment you are with others,
and no one has had to say anything, clearly
you are all just passing time. You look up
or to the side too soon to see accounts
are being taken. You will not be there
at the inventory or the disputation.
Your advocate will be weak or mildly
disinterested.
                    You were going on, they say,
about flowers and what they are and when.
You were going on about nitrogen and how
it is necessary for all life, about how

83

one moment air is just air, the next,
flower, stem, and root, this gas three parts
of all air we breathe, oxygen the other part,
its chemical symbol N, it atomic number
7. Some of this, especially the latter,
was in your head but you are certain
it was never part of what you said
to them. How this lighter than air gas
is the essential part of the green
in stem and leaf. You said that.
You were going on about splayed iron
burning in the petals, going on
about filigreed blood, blood fountains,
burnt water at the end of your hand.
Burnt water, you remember telling them that,
feeling something catch then, and you know
you are part of another story
and you will not be the teller of it.
But you go on. Turning to each of them
in some formality of generosity
you carry on so they won't be the ones
embarrassed.
                    You go on about flower
before it is flower, certainly before
it is something like verbena. You bring
your talk back to one burnt water flowing
into another burnt water, your hand
and the flower it must hold, then give away.
You tell them that it is this turning
that turns us. In your head another story
unfolds. They are telling you what you hold
is flower, a rather common one at that
in these parts, in no way starting point
for the revolution you have in mind.
There is enough here for everyone
is the appropriate response but a leap
in the talk closes the opening where
what could have been said is just lining up

as something sayable.
                    Something like that
perhaps. Something almost said perhaps that
somehow gets itself to you, catches you
in midstride not unlike the flash in the audience
the announcer warns about the danger of,
impossible to tell what senses what.
It is something perhaps as far removed
from a boy being turned by a flower as
the nutty, earth smell his father was,
but still you can bring that something
to your nerve endings daily. You can bring
it to yourself as easily as the light, clear
yellow, something like a high, clear sound
that is your lover's scent mixed with all that
sharp green air.
                    One moment you are the dancer
stretched into air, yours to move on, to hang
above. And then it is air gone simply air.
You see in that instant what it all looks like
from the house. How transparent the floor feels
even now. You are not at all sure the flash came
before the crack. You do not know what broke.
You are not even sure you're not still moving
as the curtain swings shut so near your head.
It was something like that.
                    For years you
will prepare brilliant defenses. You will
turn to history. You will study cartography.
You will speak in tongues. *Florida,*
Florianopolis, the Flores Sea, Firenze,
Florentia, Florence; bhel-3: Indo-European
root meaning *to thrive, blossom.* Probably
from *bhel-2: to blow, swell; with derivatives*
referring to various round objects and to
the notion of tumescent masculinity; blowan
florescence, folium, phullon, blom; ver-3:
Base of various Indo-European roots:

to turn, bend; werthan, to become;
flos, blostma, florin, bladaz, blaed,
bloma, bloom, blossom, *wurdam*/word,
verbum/word, verbena, blossom, *blom.*

INHABITING SEPARATE BODIES

We have always been told that wanting rises,
but here is something like longing asking
for another reading. This is not desire
if by desire we find ourselves driven toward
the edges where exacting begins to clarify itself,
where urge itself begins to set out trot-lines
for its own translations, where necessity begins
to see its own measurability.
                    This travels without sense
of strictness. It travels slowly and mostly down
with all these other bodies through paths skewed
for collision.
              All this matter
designated for travel into other matter.
The first separations a drunkenness
we call ecstacy, the shiver and tremor
of arrival before we even reach our destination.
                    Something that is other pulls
itself from our bodies. Something that is other
pulls itself into bodies, and we all lie sated
while whole plates are shifting in worlds
only our ignorance saves us from.
The geologist and the physicist would spend
the rest of their lives writing the phenomenon
up if it happened in their fields,
                    while we think we see
ourselves encased and growing, a simple miracle;
everything is in ascendance and will keep ascending,
taking us along because we are the essential part
in this whole operation, and besides
we begin to hear ourselves in these highest registers,
music in the doors between us.
                    And then it begins
to come down again, and again it comes down
in the body. This time perhaps a pain so tightly
wound it teaches us the faulty engineering

in the lower back for the first time.
The legs and feet will not propel themselves
forward, but we see little beyond
the doctor's sheet of proper lifting instructions
and how all these years we have been lifting
everything wrong and the set of pelvic thrusts
and bent knee crunches that will make our backs
strong again. And the back does mend,
before it slowly travels down again
                    and drops this time into
the chest, all of a sudden too small for all this;
too poor, to hold all those aging, contused cells
roaring in the dark cave they will never escape
from. We go to the doctors and dutifully carry
our shoulder packs home to measure the signals
the heart sends.
                    We are, at best, odd
inversions. Never the sure-footed youngster with
a full backpack hung carelessly on one shoulder.
The body given just the right tilt. The walk
so finely tuned between this place and where the feet
hit and some other place that we miss the music only
the finest ears can hear. Never the glamour girl
with her shoulder bag to match her spectator pumps,
giving her the right balance up and down and left
and right. No, we walk around with the machinery
hanging there before us like a feed bag or monitor
necessary for the interstellar travel we are about
to embark on, and we would rightly be suspicious
if anyone looked our way with unguarded admiration.
                    The diagnosis, more often
than not, is *palpitations,* and we feel a bit silly
that we alarmed everyone with our cries of "Wolf!
Wolf!" and we dutifully walk the walk prescribed.
Then so slowly we hardly remember when it all began,
the limbs and extremities go on and on,
                    the dull pain falling
into them. They sing *desire* and *parting* and how

early on these two lie easily in the same bed
and how it all is as happy an arrangement as
marriages ever get until we find ourselves somehow
                    all the way up here;
here, moving like moons circling the planet
of whatever your matter and my matter make,
never able to move any closer to whatever
has this pull on us and will not let us go,
never able to read the something we know is written
there if only we could bring the right light to it,
before we begin to sense recession, the sweet descent
we have come to recognize the way we recognize our hands,
our feet, the face that falls in the field
where we look for ourselves. We sail past,
are comforted by this configuration memory tells us
we once took for ourselves, called by our very name.

SARAJEVO, AUGUST 22, 1993

Her face is lighted.
Her reddish-golden hair
like the brilliant discs around the faces
of the old holy figures.
Her back is straight in the crookedness
surrounding her.
She stands behind men and women
old before their time.
In the broken church for Sunday services
they sit very close to one another.
Their offerings are their own faces
cracked by sniper fire.
Their eyes rest momentarily in their sockets,
brief respite from all that scanning,
all that surveillance the eyes know
they must bring to the streets.
These new ways of having to see.
These new ways of not seeing.
This new way of running faster than your body
knows how.
This other new way of running —
you are not moving fast but your body configures
running. Perhaps this is what you must do now
to save yourself. Find newer and newer ways
of running through these fires.
            This child is Velázquez's child,
the blonde one in the center of *Las Meninas.*
Sometimes when she is out to gather water
for her sisters, she thinks she sees something
of the street, something of the house
which was home when the old painter visited
there. The queen of the old masterwork
flits through her dreams now and then,
but she cannot remember who that woman is
in spite of her queenliness,
and in the daytime she never thinks of her.

She is one of Goya's children.
They will finally get us. Maybe tomorrow,
maybe next week. We will be running
for bread or oil for the stove
and one of them will find me
in the light of one of the street fires,
some street light will be the lantern that pins me.
The bullets are crazed with desire for me
in this moment. They will take me anyplace —
in the heart, in the back, in the head.
Some engorgement will find release in me,
will be glutted, will be stupefied,
but only for the time it takes me to fall
out of the light. Then it will be hungry again,
start its prowl again.
Each new ravenousness hungry with its own hunger,
sated only by its own wild gorge.

This child is Botticelli's child.
This child is one of Balthus' virgins.
This is de Saint Phalle's child. She is covered
with colored glass fragments. She is covered
with fragments of mirrors. You will see yourself
in pieces in this child.

In this child Frida Kahlo buried
her three children.

Giotto gathered colored earth in baskets
to make this angel child.

This is your mother's child.

This is the child you were, the child
who comes into your dreams to visit with you,
to love you now. When she leaves
you in the morning, you are lonely
and you long for something you cannot name
slipping from you again
and again throughout the day.

You will go to sleep for this child.

This is the child you will be son of.
This is the child you will be daughter for.

She will build a city in you, this child.
        It will start in this broken tower.
She will be standing behind you.
You will be looking for light,
your eyes will be tired, your skin will burn,
you will be beyond wanting
and you will turn. You will see this child
and she will see you.
        You will see the cartographer's compass
and the cartographer's rule; astrolabes and ink pots,
the drafting charts on the walls and on the drawing tables.
You will see the fires of invisible cities burning.
You will see the pale rose in the stone
she found for you in the quarry in the high mountains,
the silks they will sell in your marketplace,
the olive groves all along the Adriatic coast
and on the islands off the coast.
        There will be no shrines , no temples here
for many, many years. You will make what you call prayer
in the old groves.
        You will make new gardens for laughing children
who will know the architecture of things that rise
from the ground by climbing them.
        You will make new gardens for crying children
who will know morphologies by reaching for things
with their hands,
by holding these things to their mouths,
by pressing through the sweetness of things
for whatever is inside,
the way you see what you love in many ways
before you swallow it. This is the way she will see you,
this child, the moment before she flies into you.

PUTTING WILLIAM TO SLEEP

for William Bourque Turley, bn February 11, 1992

He puts his index finger and his middle finger together
when he loves you with his hands
or when he is touching meaning into things
he is bringing himself to for the first time.
The thumb and the other fingers fold
over the mysteries in his palm.
It is some kind of sacred gesture he has carried
into this new world where nothing has a name yet.
He is touching the thumbnail on my left hand
as I stand swinging him in the hammock
I have made for him of dark and arms,
of chest, of cricket sounds outside and smells
inside clothes and skin and room and house.
I sing to him of orchids in rain forests
and how they touch everything around them like that.
He could be that kind of orchid lover,
I sing to him. I sing to him of loving
by brushing holiness against everything
he comes to and everything that comes to him.
He presses the skin on my shoulder near my neck
just barely and then his hand slides down.
His whole arm is loose and heavy, falling with him —
his benedictions now for some other darkness, some
other namelessness he might grow to imagine, loving
that it always waits for him in the dark, loving
that it always waits for him on the other side.

JAMIE WALKING

for Jamie Darrell Reiss, bn April 13, 1992

1

My first daughter's gift to me, naming
her first born. His second name from
darling. I cannot remember my parents
leaving their carefully watched posts
long enough to have connected me
to the disarming angel in my name.
But surely, I tell myself, early on
they were shaken by this new thing
they had made. Surely, somewhere,
embedded deep within them —
   my mother, whose legs are stilled now
and will worry with her to the end
(my wife read in a book somewhere
that this worry is her way of loving us):
   my father, over twenty years
lying in his small granite house
on a Louisiana prairie —
surely somewhere embedded deep within
them is the small, happy leaping
the heart leaps when something *darling*
crosses its path.

2

Jamie's eyes are the blue of the sky
this morning over the Mediterranean
in the south of France, blue that comes
to water and to sky when water and sky
say to the eye holding them *I am here*
almost transparent. I am here.
This is the color I make myself
to please you. This is the color
I make myself to pull you in to me.
This is the color I love you best in.
This is the color you will not walk
straight in.

3

It was in Jamie's legs I first saw
myself. His feet beg the ground
for those instantaneous rootings
and unrootings we travel by.
His feet and legs have negotiated some
reasonable contract with the solid planes
under them. He pushes toward a start
and whirls, keeps falling over, being carried
backwards or askew by other pulls, down
by the earth that wants to hold him still,
loves him still too much to wholly let him go.
But once his clear eyes see the cats
at the back door, there is no stopping him —
the happy drunk who lurches toward the light.
Maybe this time he will be able to dive
into them as he seems to have imagined
yesterday as he went to them laughing
and calling *cat, cat, cat,* checking
with everyone in the room to see
if he had this operation under control.
Maybe this time he can hold himself steady
long enough with this invisible guideline
for them to dive into him. Maybe this time
he can deliver himself to the right place,
the color of his eyes spreading into a blue
even these baffling cats can manage love in.

WASHING CLOTHES

The French have a word for the likes of me,
blanchisseur.
But standing naked in my room
before the small white porcelain bowl,
I am whitening nothing.
It is not paling I am after here.
I am bowing to these rags
my body sang today's songs to.
I have my hands and half my forearms
in this water mixed with oils and skin
my body is finished with in this life.
I have my hands and forearms
in the smells that all day sang
like the ring-necked doves here
this is you and you and you and you and you.
We are all in this sink together
before we slip off to the underworld
for the night. This wet rite.
This weighing down with water.
This red shirt. These dark green pants.
This heavy hanging.
This last light drunk, the dew at dawn.
These colored blocks on bright blue shutters.
This dancing in the window at daybreak.
This calligraphy of fibers and air.
This invitation the rags extend
to come back, to be inside them once again.

LIGHT WITNESS

after scenes from the film *For a Lost Soldier*

My sister is hanging clothes in the rain.
It is night and I am crying,
screaming at her that she ruined the film,
that I would never have the photograph,
that he had become my friend.
How would I remember him when he went
back to wherever he had come from?
How would I know what he looked like?
How would I be able to remember
that when he saw us lined up
for the picture taking, he broke away
from his friends and into our line
to stand next to us?
How would I remember if I could not see
that he had put his arm around me,
his right hand on my upper right arm
as we stood and smiled
for the other soldier to take the picture?
This is the way the soldiers touch
each other in their pictures.
He had made me one of them
when he put his arm around me like that.
Now, I was saying to her, I can still feel
his hand on my arm. Now,
I still hear his friends calling his name,
the name with the three heavy sounds,
each sound as heavy as stone pushed
through frozen ground in the spring.
I can still hear him talking to me about hands
as we sat in the farmhouse
he and the other soldiers lived in,
about what artists make with hands like these.
I can still hear his low voice
saying that to me right now,

but in a week from now, a month, a year,
when I am his age, how will I remember
he said all that, and that he said,
the hands make what the mind sees
if I cannot see him anymore?
How will I remember riding the bike
on the path through the low wetlands
to see him if I cannot see
where I am going anymore, if I cannot smell
the air with him in it,
if I cannot see the lightness
he went away from us in?
How will I know how to play with the scarecrow
he put in the picture if the scarecrow is in my head
scaring everything away,
if I cannot get into my head to take it out
so it does not scare him away,
so we do not scare him away
because none of us can see him anymore?

FRENCH LESSON

he places his tongue just right
in his mouth
he readies his ear for what he wants
to hear
he studies the way the French move
their hands, their heads,
how they carry stomach, butt
how they engineer the slowest movements
of the hips
he will try to remember
that all things that begin in love
begin in the body
today he will write a poem
with *chasseresse* in it
he will feel the word plumb
to his toes
he will feel it course through
the top is his head
scramble back inside him
go straight for the trap door
at the back of his throat

ADAGIO

Through palm and fern
the sun shot green
beyond his French doors,

laid it at his feet
and draped his white walls.

He could not remember now
what is was
she said on her way out.
She threw Neruda's *Twenty Love Poems
and a Song of Despair* at him.

It was at his feet
rising with the green
and the adagio
she put on the phonograph
before they had begun.

It had been that sudden then,
like green air in hothouses
when one more breath will bring
darkness and you see yourself

in the going down waiting on lists
of all you pulled down with you,
your heart burrowing in the loam
as someone tallies what you owe.

MY MOTHER'S RIGHT FOOT

1

In the photograph with your three oldest children
your auburn hair is pulled neatly over rats.
Your blue gabardine suit is unwrinkled.
The lapels lie perfectly on your breast,
the embroidered piping around the cutwork in them
almost lost in the camera's differentiations of light.
I imagine the seams in your nylons curved
along your calves only as slightly as the curve
in your carefully made eyebrows.
Your feet are slim trout in your black pumps.
The child on your lap holds your hand
in her lap. Slightly opened, it could be
a hand holding an orb in another century.
I sit lower than you, but I touch
your right knee. The child on the left
is the only figure touching no one.
She is already the serious child.
Her play clothes have been passed down
and she will never get them back.
She is the imploring brown-haired maiden
in Velázquez's *Las Meninas*, leaning to the favored
one who thinks she is princess, not maid,
who lets her sister hold her hand, but barely,
who turns her blond face away from her sister's words
Where are my things?
Where is our mother now?

2

Today, your right foot hangs from the wheelchair.
It won't stay on the footrest like the other one,
curls inward like the feet of chickens hanging
on nails on the back porch waiting to be plucked,
like the freak chicken in our yard dragging a third foot.
Without drawing too much attention to yourself,
you carefully slip your hand under your knee
and lift. You bring it to the metal rest
where it stays for a while, then falls, hangs
again, takes back its curl just off the floor.
On most days it's all no more than brushing
the hair from your eyes, but on other days
that foot brings worse weather than we've had
in years, brings each day more pain than you've ever had
before, and when I lean to kiss you goodbye, it whispers
I want to talk to you about your faith.

3

This tongue is an ancient tongue.
Calling itself, at least once as I heard it then,
the mangled remnant of the queen of heaven.
The rest is litany or accounting, I can't tell which.
Like my great-grandmother on her knees
in the middle of the afternoon in the center of the house
praying aloud *Mère de la reine du ciel, priez*
pour nous. Bonne sainte Anne, prenez pitié
de nous. Mère de la reine de ciel, priez pour nous.
Then it says something about a bull or bulls
in the back pasture. I am coming home,
the knees of my pants blood-soaked.
We have spent the afternoon dehorning cattle,
holding their heads close to the ground
as the men placed long-handled shears
to the base of the horn and snipped,
releasing the first rush of blood onto the straw-covered,
shit-covered ground. When we let them go,
they shook their heads back and forth
sending blood in arcs. Over their heads
and over ours, a rain we were caught in
over and over again all afternoon. We starting it.
We cursing it. We, befouled. We, amazed, ourselves,
the arcs going each time away from us
until we so wanted it again that without prompting
from the men we took the next animal to the ground,
held its head there.

I am in the same dehorning yard
and the animals are smaller this time.
We throw the young bull calves to the ground,
cleaner, quicker work. Getting the belly up, working
our hands and knees, spreading the hind legs,

reaching down into the lower belly for the small, hard knots,
holding everything up for the man snapping
the thick rubber ring in place
and then letting the young one go.

To get at the new feeling the young bulls begin high
in the haunches, their skin like rippled water
moving down and into this new, tight nerve.
Back hooves pull to the tight nerve, too, each calf
an old vaudevillian tap dancing his way
into the back pasture. Like the good audience,
we punch at each other and try to fill the yard
with the laughter of a whole choir of castrati.

I am in another yard. We are cutting still.
In the morning our father and our uncles
held perfectly the knives on the stone wheel.

Here, these men are quiet and gentle. Like lovers they take
the pig's scrotum in their hands, bring the hardened masses
to the surface for one quick slice and then another.
They know the sharpness of their knives and put them down
as I take a piece of sheeting to soak the wound.
Only then the sound of blood and steel and coal oil
tearing the air.

Under the oak my mother is telling me about chickens
with the pip. She points them out, tells me of crust
in the throat and on the mouth and what must be done.
I am tying them upside down, hanging them from a low branch.
She doesn't tell me how I am to do what I have to do.
I am trying to bat their heads off.
I know something is wrong here but I not stop.

4

I am wearing necklaces of heads and horns.
I am gathering bull nuts and pig testicles.
I have more than twelve baskets full.
I see the bull from the back pasture from the beginning
        of this dream.
I see the contest designed for me.
I know never to call a woman's tongue the mangled voice
        of anything.
I am in Crete dancing.
I am going over the bull's head.
I am a young Roman woman. I am Perpetua.
I ask again and again *When are we to be tossed?*
I am in Mesopotamia. I may be the king's lover.
One of us will not come out of this thing alive
        and the other will tell of it.
I am trying to find the talking foot.
I am trying to say *beloved.*
I am trying to keep the baskets from spilling.
I am trying to keep my necklaces on.
I am saying I know this story.
I am saying I know these people.
I am calling beloved the curves in my mother's arch.
I am calling blessed the arcs of blood.
I am saying this story is not about to end.

PHYSICS REPORT

1

       It is the end of the love bug season
here in south Louisiana.
We are taking teflon-wrapped sponges
to our windshields and to the bumpers
of our cars.
       In northern New Zealand a mountain top blows.
The ash takes with it a lake.
The water no longer identifiable
or measurable as what it was,
a deep blue bowl in thin air.
       I know more than nothing about
Lorenz's initial condition effect
on weather systems theory.
I know more than nothing about
energy field physics,
but I like the idea of poets calibrating
the energy in the lines of what they make
and scientists getting out their calipers
to measure the fat content in images.

2

        In Dixie Speyrer's sixth hour class just last week
the testosterone levels, she says, were unchartable.
It was as if some cajun blonde Medusa had turned
this boy-filled class to charged stone.
In the chronology of the narrative, three weeks after
the beginning of the fall term
Elizabeth Broussard's class schedule changed.
Ben Bernard wrote an essay
on the person who most influenced him
and he wrote about his uncle
he works with.
He said his uncle was teaching him a trade.
That it was more than learning how to be a cabinet maker.
It was about how to smooth surfaces
and how to make angles fit.
It was about how to make things
strong so that no one ever noticed
how strong a thing was.
It was about dovetails and miter boxes.
And then he said it was, too,
about how is uncle was teaching him
how to be a good father and a good husband,
and he didn't know where that last turn came from
and he wondered what connections, if any,
all that had to do with what Miss Dixie had been saying
one day about something that sounded foreign to him
that you couldn't do when you write,
and then something about your writing
having to be about you and having to be true,
and it seemed to him that this line in his essay
about a father and a husband was both of those things
and besides that he didn't know why
he kept seeing Elizabeth about to turn

around in his writing-log entries.
Her long blond hair moving.
Her turning her face to him.
Her eyes the color of deep mountain lake water.
Him, some father, some husband,
swimming in them.

3

    Just before he closed his eyes for the last time Hokusai
released thirty-six variations of each of his
Thirty-six Views of Mount Fuji.
    This morning at the edge of a pine grove
near the emperor's retreat the mist barely touches
the tops of the boulders in the garden.
The caretaker is raking the gravel.
The imperial embroiderers are taking notes
on the pinks in the peonies blooming
next to winding, leafless paths.
    A hummingbird near the rim of the Atchafalaya Basin
is making its way to the red mallows,
the subscription in its wings
            Kyoto, Kyoto, Kyoto
the hurried aria its heart sings
            yokuboo, yokuboo, yokuboo.

From *Burnt Water Suite*

1999

THE GATE

It's not falling
anymore that bothers me.
In the years since we were at the gate,
I've fallen from greater heights.
I've worked on falling.
I've fallen in love with falling,
can pull in and roll with the best.
I took tumbling lessons, learned
to jump from planes, turned
falling into minuet and waltz.
I played football for the falling
and the refusal to fall.
When I run, I imagine myself tripping
myself, a kind of daily practice,
a *kata* of sorts, me taking myself down
with one foot, rolling out
of the other's runners' way
and coming up again
without so much as breaking the breath's
rhythm.

It's not falling.
*You are coming to me
in the side yard. You pick me up.
You put your grandson on the gate,
tell him you are giving him a ride.
You shake the gate from under him.
He falls.*

It's not falling.
The Jax-beer smell on your breath
and in your clothes is sweet.
I never believed you didn't mean to
give a boy a good ride.
Your dry, scaley, uremic hand,
your cirrhotic-widened girth,

your yellow face
were the only you I knew
and they all said *love, love, love,*
even as you became the horse
you pushed. Love pushing
harder and harder for me
on your back, *love,*
as your heavy breath caught me.

It's not falling.
It's all the drunkenness
in the spin on the way down
and in the afterlife,
catching your hook in my mouth,
beginning somewhere near the gate
to breathe your breath.
This had nothing to do with knowing
anything. It was a natural thing,
not like taking lessons to learn
to follow one breath with another
breath. It was a natural thing,
like breathing in water
for what seems like eternal time,
then being hit,
then the new air,
then breathing your breath
as a way of finding my way
to you and to the dizzy path
you walked your whole life
through.

GETTING THE TULIPS IN

Masha says *If I lived in Moscow,*
I should not mind what the weather
was like. Happy people don't notice
whether it is winter or summer.
Her enameled onion tops rise. Blue.
Ocher. Some the color of old blood.
She has her gardener digging on all fours.
The curves in his glasses catch sweat,
blur his world too as he goes
to the ground to make these globes
for his mistress — clear yellows,
satin-glass reds, fleshy, undulant pinks.
She stands apart on early spring's still hazel
lawn dreaming a sky filled with Easter eggs
from Byzantium saying to Vershinin
Happy people don't notice whether
it is winter or summer. If I lived
in Moscow, I should not mind
what the weather was like.

DÜRER'S HARE

In some catalogues Dürer's hare is listed
simply *Hare* and in others *Young Hare*.
That distinction is not an important matter
here. Look at the way she sits there
as you so often do lost in large internalities.
Aged beauty may very well be enlarged perimetry,
the world outside itself dwarfed, a natural drift,
involute, congested majesty scored as diminution.
Those eyes seek nothing as far as we can tell.
There is nothing from without can make anything of fear.
She sits so nearly completely inside herself
it is as if she has become her own favorite large chair.
Look at the way her front paws know finally
how to rest. Look at the nails that have grown long
and hard. The beauty of nailness is its inherence,
onyx as natural as undependable measure of anything
to do with age, or life, or in some instances, even death.
But then go back from these indecipherables.
Look at the beautiful curve in her haunches.
Look just below the curved line to the wrinkles
that do more than suggest withering.
In this rippled texture the hair is thinning
even while it keeps its young cinnamon hues here and there.
Beauty is residuum. It never leaves where it first sits.
Look finally at that patch of color in the lower right haunch
on the left of the painting. I love the way it reproduces
differently in different renderings. It is sometimes green
or blue or purple turning to bronze. It is the bruise
I have come to look for when I first come to it.
This color field is flecked throughout the hare.
It is repeated in another field that comes to rest quietly
outside her on the other side of the painting
where it penetrates and suggests itself beyond the edge.
I see this, my love, as the bridge beyond. It is coolness
or shade she might go to if she chose to move.
In fact, this watery shadow is replacement eventually

for everything that we all are. But you, my dear rabbit,
are here tonight. Of gone, or passing, or loss,
you do not register even the slightest registration.
You are here, a gatherer for the deeper hues around you.
For now everything within the frame you have put to rest.

ALL THE THINGS YOU ARE

Les Heures Musicales de Biot
11eme Festival
Eglise Sainte Marie Madeleine

Claude Bolling in Biot

Star Dust

in the church of *Marie Madeleine*

Stomping at the Savoy

the six gold candlesticks above him

Waiting for the Robert E. Lee

– like elder cardinals
vying for the big title
– like beauty queens in lame gowns
– the pope and would-be
popes can't let it show
– the pope can't dance
in public,
even to

Tiger Rag

– it doesn't matter if Madonna
of the Foil Robe
on the altar is shaking
her skirt
– it doesn't matter if the red and
pink roses
the sodality ladies have brought
are dancing with the background
figures in the Stations of the Cross.

118

Just one of those things

                – even if Saint Billie Holiday
                and Saint Duke E. have loosened
                   the plaster in the cherubs
                over the paintings on the right
                wall and one of those cherubs
                is finally getting up courage
                   to ask what he now seems to have
                   wanted for a very, very long time
                – just one dance *s'il vous plaît* with

Sweet Georgia Brown

                who
                has always lived on the other side
                of the arch stretching over the
                huge holy painting,
                that arch they have straddled
                all their lives

I know that you know

                he says to her in a low voice
                somewhere in your stone heart, the

Echoe of spring

                and she acquiesces finally
                as they go off in a

Handful of Keys

Dancers in love

                swinging in the air above
                to

Nice work if you can get it

        And everybody in the church *aprés*
        fait le

Boogie-Woogie on the St. Louis blue

        le maestro tells us at that point
        to join him,
        to
        – *snap, snap, snap* –
        our fingers when he gives the signal
        and almost immediately my friend
              Lynda Frese sings,
        her voice soprano-silver tinged
          with violet she saw this morning
        in the asparagus in the market,
        she sings from the deepest room
        in her heart *I've never snapped*
        my fingers in church before –

              I have never been told I could do this
              before
              and the god in the marble
              baldacchino he lives in
              on the altar
              joins her

        tonight he is the village tenor
        who trained his voice tending animals
        in the pale air in the mountains
        near here
              he cries I could die now
        and young Raymond throws shyness

              and popes in somersaults
              over his head
              he asks the school's director to
              dance

                    he will not be conscious
                    for some time now
                    his face is even-colored,
                    his teeth and the skin around his eyes
                    laughing
          our friend Tanner is teaching
          his business students some 15th c.
          folk dance
          (he tells me later how it was like a
          miracle, how he knew instantaneous-
          ly, how he had this feeling that it
          had waited all these years for this
          music and this flesh to dance it)
          quand Claude a commence a notre round
          de

Nice work if you can get it

          and then everyone in the church
          is dancing
          even *Marie Madeleine*
                    has quit asking to wash feet
                         she's in her older skin
          on the floor now wondering
          why she ever gave up belly dancing
          half the people in the church
          are mouthing into the nearest ear
          a whispering song

Nice work if you and get it

          and the sung to are whispering back
               and you can get it if you try
               and you can get it, baby, if you try

The Blue Boat

Complete
2004

I

On a appris à écouter
tout ce que la chaleur peut engendrer,
tout ce que l'amour peut accoucher.

APPLES, THE BLUE PLATE, AND PHYSICS

Three yellow apples on a dining room table
in south Louisiana do not suggest cataclysm,
not even emergence of anything discernible
necessarily. But when my wife moved them
from the center to the quadrant near the window,
the window exploded. The world was almost all
arboretum and frost. Matisse was singing
the blue you see on your computer screens
into this world we live in. Bonnard was pulling
us to the bathroom where we could look with him
at his wife who was bathing there and telling
us that he planned to paint everything he knew
of water in the transparency of color rising
over kneecaps, thighs; the fold and curve
of hip and belly calling him to continualities
he could not name with any kind of certainty
so he called them *bath, water, apple, wife*.

CLEANING THE MARTIN HOUSES EACH SPRING

It is what the garden asks that matters.
Enclosure arises out of its first interrogatories.
A child's bicycle path, a cow's, it utilizes,
or a rabbit's to its warren, the way eyes

eventually move toward the large palm
in the ferns, the way the heart is calmed
by a line set out and then realized.
Both my grandmothers' gardens were tied

to the outside world by long graveled paths
we could hear ourselves on before
we came to the quiet inside their gardens.

Each of them had some vine clinging to laths
in lattices confounding the idea of line even more,
not unlike heart plied by rhymed returning martins.

THE ENCLOSURE THE GARDEN IS

from detail of Sa'di's *Darius and the Garden*
from Buston's *Garden of Perfume*
Iran, Safavid period, 1522–1523

After the hurricane we went out into the garden to see the lemons
and how they fared. Our hearty Meyer lemons hang like lights
against their darker green scaffolding, light itself for birds
to perch in — cardinals, yellow-bellied finches, jays for hours
exercising torment on all around them. A fine covering of ashes
will fall, the sky taking our burnt offering of felled trees. Our skins
will redden from this close work with fire. In Darius' garden skins
are largely the subjects of the miniature — the central color-field, ashen
to deepen lapis in a king's saddle blanket, his persimmon robe. Hours
he and his men will hunt, milk mares, let foals suck amid the birds'
songs. In the foreground the young boy's heart is much lightened;
he is content to press the mare's head and neck to his. The lemon-
robed roper in the upper left is his foil. Here are contented days of
creature and leaf enclosed, king and herdsmen loafing in *pairi-daēza*.

EMBARKATION

after Watteau

It is mid-October and Venus shines in
the morning sky again. Desire
is a door inside your heart keeps wanting to open
first, confuted brilliance you will never tire

of. Lust or something like it can burn like sin,
or it can be the holy coal to lead you to the purling fires
the prophets are always led to in the end.

Truth all too often lies a recumbent serpent amid confusion
of truculent tongues. Expectancy sidles. Even strife
has to beg for its own life. Darkness and reluctant shadow motion

possibility of shape, contour both our steerage and our suspiration.
Specularia perfoliata is Venus' looking glass. My wife
tends to these small blue stars in our garden, planetary fibrillation
she calls them, her protection from knowing too well how to live her life.

THE WHITE GEESE ON THE LAWRENCE RANCH

Someone has relocated seven white geese on the Kiowa Ranch
in northern New Mexico, put them in the side yard, made it
their song yard on this elevated ground, the place theirs
to waddle in and sing if they want to in empty goose hours
next to the largest building in the remote little compound.
Today the earth wobbles in its course as it must surely have
always. Some say it is such wobble creates most miraculous
disorder. It is snowing in Mexico this summer, and the snow
in the Cascades is not melting on time to open the trails.
Pepper farmers in New Jersey will get next to nothing
for their crops failing in dry fields. Nearly everything
will have to be plowed under. Three boys in New Mexico
are separated from other hikers on the Tesuque Trail
north of Santa Fe. The headlines read "Three Boys Rescued
in the Rain," the rain as large a part of news here
as anything. Wobble brings water to this clean, thin air,
colors sky a blue so deep one would think it is the bay
at Corinth one is looking into on this mountain rising
from the high desert floor. Everything else here is just
as it should be. The resident sage seems to lie still
in the smallest part of his remains in the little shrine.
The tiny work cottages present themselves to us restored.
Even Frieda seems quiet, lying there with her Italian lover
as Lawrence's phoenix rises above them. Georgia O'Keeffe's
little bench is there. The plaque says it is the same bench
she brought to the base of the ponderosa pine, that it is
from this bench she saw the swirl in the branches rhymed
with the stars swirling in the night sky. The little bench
is painted green that surely resides in every green we know
but green we rarely think we see in this world we live in.
What dropped into her memory that night on her green pillow
on green ground she made into something she quietly loved
her whole long life. The little bench is in the backyard,
easy to miss unless you are looking for it or discover it
without expecting to. The geese, on the other hand,
are insistently, loudly here. They rush to the fence line

separating us from them and call, their lively gaggling
copulative transcriptions in long necks dancing like snakes
above the immaculate cluster their clumped bodies make.
It is their job to shape this music at the gate. Lawrence
is cursing inside the house in cantatory time in this music.
Frieda gives him back as good as she gets, laughing,
holding on to the post on the porch near the steps.
She turns to him, issues her one last epithet, she says.
She is a slip away from tears, and then she laughs again.
Dishes are breaking in these songs in these slender necks.
Someone is crying out. Something is making love.

PEONIES

for Terry Clay Girouard

The pink peonies in the blue glass vase impede nearly everything
going on in his head today. Five full pink globes are first and foremost
engineering, and then they are color and chemistry. Saw-toothed wings
announce themselves in the feathered edges the petals make, or ghosts

of roseate spoonbills which make their nests at the rookery in the lake
near his home. He moves them from time to time. Now on a low table
near his bed. Now in the kitchen. In western windows so they can take
in the last light of the day. All of this dancing is for the emergent stabile

he knows will surface eventually on the palette in his mixings of titanium
white and alizarine red, the hooker's green and Prussian blue to tone
things down a bit here and there. Pure-from-the-tube magenta and cadmium
red-deep for unadulterated blush and flash. In another room a phone

rings. He looks out and sees flower in the geometry of the hay balers in the fields
he's painted so many times before, unlikely flowers kindred, unlikely kin unsealed.

CATENARY

after Jasper Johns' *Catenary* series

When Jacob picked the field stone for a pillow he knew the complications
close to home. He could not have known the stratifications the morning
would bring. He was just a tired man whose mother had sent him away
to her father's land on the pretext of finding a wife. She had had enough
of Hittite women she said to her husband. Jacob's journey would be ease

to her in her old age she said too, and being a compliant husband he blessed
his son. Jacob took the blessing and left, another journey to save his life.
Like all travelers he would tire at the end of the day. The sun would set.
He would find a stone to go under his head. In the rubble night became,
he would dream his ladder, catenation of angelic escalation attended to

by his father's god and his father's father's. He would have to crawl out
of this dream or climb out of it. He chose one way; anointed the stone
itself, then the template it had become within him. He saw himself reader
of the insides of things. But even in the light of a new day he could not go
past habituations of night where he saw contentious angels and was afraid.

POSING FOR OUR FIRST COMMUNION PICTURE

The fields my father and my uncles plowed are the backdrop
for this picture. My cousin's hair is clipped close to the skin

like mine. Our ears are large flowers blooming off our faces.
My mother is wishing this cleanness she's witnessing will last,

but she knows we will tunnel our way back toward waywardness
like the goat boys we are. According to her, we will be standing

in the next frames with girls, their short red skirts occasions
of sin, if not sin itself outright. We are like birds, tethered, or

refrains in gypsy songs. Cameras will catch us again like this
against the church door before and after services. My aunt asks

when we get home for just one more. We will pause, but barely.
We hurry to the house, loosen ties we never wear, start to change.

POSTCARD FROM ITALY

from detail of Fra Angelico's *Annunciation Angel*

for Mark Doty

The angel on the postcard said it all,
or at least what I imagined
the poet could not say outright
about his beloved's dying.
"We're having to make adjustments,"
he writes, and "spring will help."
The comforts he takes are comforts
all good caretakers are prone to
take when they tend the dying.

Grief is grit and dirt. Beyond it will be bursts
of green not unlike the green crenulation
in this little Italian angel's wings.
Grief is frozen rain and snow.
Beyond it will be days succeeding days
like bright folds in the monk's curtains
or in the heavenly robes he loved to paint.

One day we pull for air inside the smoke of loss
and impending calamity. Absence seeps in everywhere.
But when the poet writes "soon will be snowless,"
he takes death for the rough jewel it is and holds it
in his hand. "Soon will be snowless," is his
annunciation of grace and plentitude tied to breach,
a thing as near complete as what the angel came to say.

WHERE LAND MEETS SKY

for Elemore Morgan, Jr.

He loves this place he's fallen into:
his skies of smeared lilac, his clouds spun
by muscled ether, congealed air so newly blue
it's hard to tell it from the sky we knew once
and loved so. After shot-silk skies, what else?
All the earth and all that's creatured in it. Tongues
of irises from the swamps, big lazy trees, bells
on boats in creeping rivers and cows like peace
flags grazing in the prairies, or lying in wells
of cow dreams making milk. He loves the creases
and the blur: stalks filled with rice to falling,
water rushing from pipes, and a leaf in wind. Leases
on anything that takes us to the places these converge,
a line in all we see and know, oh holy curve and surge.

OLD WOMEN FISHING FROM BRIDGES

There is something about dropping a line into the unseen.
Fishing we usually call it here. A mother fishes for clues
to her children's secretive lives in the piles of clothes
they relinquish to her for laundering. Another mother
occupies herself with other thoughts– too risky this
fishing. She might catch much more than she knows
what to do with. A boy fishes for the signals that keep
promising to add up to something. Another takes ends
of strings, all too willing to be the fish in these scenes.
He will let an Ariadne pull him out of the maze. Easy
work. He has only to respond to tug and taut in string.
Some fishermen don't know the first thing about waters
they fish in. Some girls fish with their eyes, use other
body parts when eyes don't work. The really bold cast
into the openness of heart, mind even. Some girls, boys
learn to fish in the wine market, others in pots on stoves.
My father-in-law liked the idea of having me in a boat
for whole afternoons. On the way out to *les Fordoches*
he pointed out the water moccasins sunning themselves
in Spanish moss clusters overhead, thick black coils
in delicate gray nests. He pointed them out on fallen trees
lying in the coffee-colored shallows at the front of his boat,
and the small alligators too sleeping in the mud flats near
the banks on either side. I saw to it that he liked the idea
only once. My mother sees fishing as the making of things.
Her table is full. The platters are steaming. Her children
are happy. My father and I filet our catches of sheephead,
redfish and speckled trout. We gut foot tubs of sac-à-lait,
bream. Fishing for my mother is an ichthyophagous dream.
But old women fishing from bridges fish mostly just for fish.

GIOTTO'S ANGELS

from Giotto's *Lamentation*
Arena Chapel, Padua, 1305–1306

I have always loved those grieving angels
in Giotto's *Lamentation*. Each one, grave
contentious rhyme for the mirrored loss
below. Giotto lets us see here and there
these were airy beings once, a robe blurs
into dark blue ether, one is held hovering
under tongues of flame. This is the angel
of things to come. The domination in this
scene though is *gravitas*, the fiery angel's
little companion makes an arch of back
and head in stiff-armed desolation, two
of them bring clasped hands to their necks
as though blood of earthly love coursed
in that holy passageway, two extend arms
from the body in a gesture making prayer
of the human heart. But these creatures,
we are told, have no heart as we know heart,
have no blood, no sex, no hands to pull up
to fleshy faces. No robes as such to bring
to the face to wipe tears from their eyes.
Yet, there they are, and here we are, wanting
to call them brother, sister, recognizing
our rent in theirs, even if they cannot be
rent. And the other peculiarity they give
witness to: on the ground their rhymed
sodality is struck with a muted airiness
they will never be used to; they do not know
where they are, or how to breathe in the heft
of sorrow in the air all around them; where
heart is, or how to hold on to the very thing
that kept them tethered to this world and to
the very lives they had just begun to love so
before this last disconsolate leap let them go.

MONDAY'S SONG

My sisters were sent out early
with clothes in bundles as large
as clouds. They took soap with them,
and bluing. They knew for hours
they were consigned to the wash house
and its fringes. I went to the yard
with cuttings, rootings, and divisions.
It was my job to make beds, to edge
and line the green with flags and mallow,
with phlox and four o'clocks,
seven sisters roses for backdrop,
wisteria in the reckless ground,
magnolia fiscata and Russian olive
and large waxy gardenias leaking
their wild perfumes, mimosas
and *soleil d'or* and hydrangeas
and everything else aunts brought
in bags and boxes and sacks,
everything my grandmothers thought
we should try in a yard younger
and infinitely sadder than theirs.
We all had our Monday tasks
and my mother's was to sing songs
she carried over from yesterday.
She sang them best alone
as she went down on hands and knees
to scrub the green and white linoleum
tiles in her small, dark kitchen.
It was as though she had to separate
herself from us, needed our distance
to help her with pitch and volume.
Kyrie eleisons inside the spading
and the staking, inside shirtsleeves.
Agnus Dei in sheets as large as sails
in the side yard. *Sanctus* filling pillow-
cases, *sanctus* blessing all the casements.

Sanctus to the edges of our property,
trembling in treelines and in hedgerows,
trembling down the bright green stalks
of the four o'clocks to their tubers
large as small childrens' arms, trembling.

MY FATHER AT GRAND ISLE

Whoever took this picture of my father loved him.
He is a boy still, but barely. He has separated himself
from all others he came here with at this watery retreat
his mother takes her family and friends and her priest
to in the summers. That is, everyone except this one
who gazes up at him leaning into the world, held back
by the railings on the balcony. Everything behind him
is a blur so that we cannot see details in the structures.
What we can see though are the edges of the wide gulf,
placidity itself objectified in this captured light. It is
mostly this broad blankness this boy will grow toward.
There are no sailing boats in the wide expanse of water.
There are no cities in the distance, nor horses running
across the turf in the mottled light the camera catches
too. It will not be something we will have to accustom
ourselves to, calling him Father. None of us have seen
him in this picture yet. None of us have had the chance
to cling to the boy in it about to slip into the unexpected
curve he is shaping in this quiet moment definitively his.

HOKUSAI'S GREAT WAVE

from *Mount Fuji Seen Below a Wave at Kanagawa* from
Thirty-six Views of Mount Fuji, Katsushika Hokusai, 1760–
1849

for Hiroshi and Kitty

Hokusai's great wave is not about time.
There is snow in this scene, but not snow
of winter. Of course, the scene could be set
close to winter, just no way one can surely tell.
There are no cherry trees in blossom, those symphonies
of trees, whole and quarter notes, half notes and 16th notes
all blooming in concert. There is no rust in the maple trees.
There is no white light of mid-summer,
nor any courtesans stripped to the waist
in that brief time in the day that is mostly theirs unless
some rich merchant wants them for the pouring of his tea,
or for some other use. They are not mopping their moist necks
with thin white scarves, nor the dripping flesh under their breasts,
or pushing tendrils of wet hair away from their faces.
It could be either morning or afternoon,
but there is no clear definitiveness there either —
only the unfathomable surge of dark blue wave and spume,
Mount Fuji in the background, still and insistent as ancestral presence.
It is finally all those little men pulling fiercely
which delight and surprise us, those little boats
as light as husks, the grand physics of proximities.

COMPOSITION IN YELLOW AND BLUE

from *The Lacemaker, c. 1669–1670*, Jan Vermeer

*If two circles are painted respectively yellow and blue,
brief concentration will reveal in the yellow a spreading
movement out from the center, and a noticeable approach
to the spectator. The blue, on the other hand, moves in
upon itself, like a snail retreating into its shell, and draws
away from the spectator.*
— *Concerning the Spiritual in Art*, Wassily Kandinsky

If her hands moved they would move like lively birds
perhaps, those little rapid shifts and starts deep muscle
answers to, the dance of flesh and skin girded
to the call of making things — bread, lace, or love hustled
into corners, notes, or beds. All this could be hers
she knows. The lace her little fingers often muzzled
had it way of telling her things — another light, another air, curded
love, all its excesses, all she could desire of chucking and nuzzling.

But here she is content to make something else of the hours.
Her eyes turn away from the gush of white thread and red
spilling itself on the table from her pillow cushion. Bowers
far outside her window block no light, pie no face or head.
Time gives all its various ashen hues. But flower flowers here within —
concentration's captive & its spread light lemon dress, collar, bobbins, pins.

A WOMAN CLINGS TO THE IDEA OF WHAT MIGHT HAVE PASSED FOR LOVE AND WHAT SHE HOPES MIGHT COME TO PASS AGAIN

after Leon Stokesbury and Vermeer

She reads the whole note once again.
We can tell it is winter from the ermine-
lined jacket she wears indoors. In the morning
when he left he left his scent inside the rain-

dampened air. She was a kind of woman
who could cling to, if she had wanted, greater things —
a reputation in the town for some good use, omen

prophesying beneficence that would come her way, a string
of pearls a painter had tried to give her strung onto yellow ribbon.
But his pale husk she has in her hands, now thin

and fair reminder of sacrament live flesh retains.
In this city by the sea one is encouraged to learn to read winds.
She puts the letter away, has a fleeting thought about wages of sin,
and then she reads the whole note once again.

CHICKEN TREES AND BAMBOO GROVES

Danny Lyons stopped to say he was worried about the tallow trees,
that once those chicken trees took root no rescuer would ever stay

their capricious takeover. He didn't use the word *capricious*, rather
he stalled over some other word skewed on the scaley contusions

within him, something that felt to him like reversal of large purpose
he was in charge of when already he knew he had barely enough time

to do what he had to. He brought his foot to the tractor brake, bailed
himself out of his seat and hobbled his way into an old bamboo grove

where I had passed the morning listening to the crickets making songs
out of the most rudimentary sounds, leg rubbings put to use of shrill

music. I almost talked to him of leaves, posteriority and diminishment
in relation to loam production, low shrubbery and thickets in relation

to the architecture of rabbit warrens, the way these very trees turn rusty,
purple and golden in autumn, inflame the very world we live in, ways

one might scan the teals bobbing on the pond or egrets on a bare branch.
But we never got to any of that. Him just seeing me at some inexplicably

triangulated pause in the woods like that left him with only the stupefying
catch basin of a thought that anyone would want to save Chinese tallow

trees for anything, or bamboo. The air he walked away in had the heft of slate,
and his tractor idled on the roadside like a tired cantor practicing weary notes.

LA TOUSSAINT

after Sei Shonagan

It was on a cloudy morning on the first day of the eleventh month.
On my morning run, twice the sun broke through
and then the clouds filled the sky again.
The leaves on the trees in the forest were losing their green
but they would never turn gold and red and purple
in this part of the world.
I was stopped suddenly by a red pine snake
that had made its way from the edge of the road
in this unseasonable heat.
As I left a beauty that I still feared there on the ground,
my father came to me through the clouds.
I asked the old monosyllabist how it was up there
in his heaven.
"The good thing," he said, "is that you don't have to speak.
Something within you, large before it ever shapes itself
as a simple yes or no, is sufficient here.
The bad thing is that everything is tending toward something else.
It is like living in air."

THE FORTUNE TELLER IN THE CAMARGUE

Bulls the geography is noted for, white
horses, gypsies and flamingoes rightly
there too; and a voice of governance —
I see you happiest in a dimmed light
among birds. But you want wind
and sun on your skin. You see
your work, you say, in moving out
of shade. You imagine yourself
in citrus groves — those lemons
that do so well in the warm air
you live in — Louisiana Sweet
oranges, Key limes, blood oranges,
and Ruby Reds, as you call them.
Those might be yours as citron hours
ashen their own yellow-green light.
But, you will lose yourself, wind
mostly in paths of darkening cedars.
From here you will not be without.
It will be home the way some shelves
on sea floors are homes for Lemnos,
others not. Often unsuspecting air
is the needle's eye sweetness
travels in. You will want oranges
above every other thing until slim
darting martins bring in the martin hour
and you will fall in love with flight
like theirs, not have to choose or slight
neither one bright thing or another.

THE LIE IN THE COMFORT OF WATER BIRDS

after Ravel's *Gaspard de la nuit*

When we were being told our first stories,
we were told the fabrication of lies
would be called storytelling. It is necessity
of understanding light lets contradictions in
such as these. Calm and comfort are neither
simple things. All calm is gentle storying,
unmalicious lie we use to carry us along.
The air, for instance, seen as this blue slate
before us is one lie if we see it separate
from sky. The homeliness of pelicans is lie
to one who has seen three of them above water
rise; first, two ascending, the other joining
two measures later, and then all three piercing
the water, a small study in conjunctive grace.
The soothing creak of a solitary water bird
is only part of the story. It is itself
a small withholding. The ear not hearing
continuo in the lapping the water makes
does not hear true. The sounds the land bird
sings back near the shore is rhymed copulative.
The locust's high register is instillation
in air. These are sounds the year lingers in
as it moves from the bright fullness of late summer.
But lie or lull, whatever we come to name
progression usually begins where calm lies.
Just let me call for witness, my love, only these
configurations and my deposition will be complete.
See Venus as those rich Florentines saw her.
She rides all calm in a pink shell over green water.
This shell later pilgrims will attach to the lapels
of a traveling cloak, to the upturned brims of hats.
Shell as designation of being pulled like thread
through beads of holy sites. And as often as not
the farthest shore for many will mark the end

of pilgrimage toward perturbed grace. But she
is barely marked by the fierce expiration
from the west. It moves her to the flowery robe
the hour holds for her. She will take it on
as she takes on the sea. What it is she is
and where she is going, repositional vestigium.
Look for the small blue forget-me-nots in de Heem's
large vases. Are they not diminutive anchor
for every other blue amidst the striped, stippled
intoxicants of everything that is not blue?
Pick any one of Utamaro's babies drunk on mother's milk.
In one of these prints a mother holds her baby's face
next to hers. She has the infant poised above a bowl
of its own bath water. The child gazes into the double
image, nascence and what it has miraculously separated
itself from. This is the moment of interregnum.
It is the calm in the face of everything it will become.

CLAIRE, SONNET AFTER SURGERY

She's ninety, so I called to see how she was doing
and she said she thought she was alright;
there was still that Saint Teresa doll spewing
nonsense and a chicken hanging above her bed all night.

When I asked her if the chicken could be the Paraclete,
she said she didn't think so, that it was more the kind
of bird she could make a meal with, something complete

with yams and oyster dressing, and if she could find
where she put them, those little Parker House rolls, and sweet
Italian ices for dessert. What was "bothering her mind"

though were all those molls flat-foot floozying and endlessly cooing
about how it was always rougher than you thought it might
be to fly to the moon, that she still had unbelievable sewing
to finish; and that holy chicken, angel unreachable, was still alight.

COURTYARD AT INNSBRUCK CASTLE

after Dürer

Water never completely leaves the walls here.
There's never quite enough heat in the rooms.
In the little yellow apartment near the far tower
with its gothic entryway, the newlyweds love
the spare way the light enters their little room.
They love the way when the sun does appear,
it tears away the shadow world, gets itself inside
the mahogany brew within the leaded decanter
on the little bedside table and shines from there.
How it paints the outside windows, the outside
world itself sometimes in windows' reflections
on the blank surfaces a jug might become in one
illuminated moment such as this one is. Some
wedding gift for these two needful of reminder
and reflection of the outside world they could so
easily do without these days. They fall in love
with something near almost hourly, angle and
descent of light on the polished wood, a keyboard
on the far wall, virginal she might go to for music
if they could ever get out of bed for sustainment
of the sort that would include made harmonies.
For a few moments, or even for a month or two,
they might keep this small Tyrolean space theirs,
and as empty of others as only lovers can manage.
Tomorrow the sky may even turn blue. People
might walk through the squares and in the streets.
The priest may suddenly appear in the small pulpit
window near the church with pronouncements and
promulgations. There will be a fishmonger surely
and birds will be sold in cages. A charwoman or
man will have work to do. The banker will feel for
the heft of his wealth. The cartographer's delivery
will be delivered. Someone will move certainly
toward final rites. There will be appropriate flurry.

And the wheelwright is late, rushes to his job too,
past the old gardener tending the *Grüss en Aachen*.
They will all have to wait though for another time.
Today, the lovers have cast spells on this little town.
They plan to keep things for forever just as they are.
And that failing, for as long as the money holds out.

MARTHE AND HER DOG

after Bonnard

It was not the sky he was interested in
if the paintings are any indication
of interest at all. It seems too much
was going on inside. All that water
in those tiled bathrooms, indolence
on a bed that stretches the ends
of the canvas. Those volatile fruit
in plates and in baskets, that fruit
going to ripeness, heat and sugar
turning to shadowy water under them,
incendiaries on the large white tables
they sit upon. Figures caught barely
in the scene so that we doubt
whether they are clearly, intentionally
figures at all. And yet what are those
shapes at the edges, and at the edges
all the other blurrings we lean toward?
Even when he went outside with Marthe,
he makes us believe he is standing near
her, so close that he could hear
what the dog has come to her to hear.
Il y a des jours, mon petit chien,
c'est seulement un chien, qu'une femme
peut parler avec. This is a dog
who clearly loves her. He is the dog
who sits on the floor near the tub.
He waits for her to emerge from watery
reverie that habitual bathers immerse
themselves in. In this scene, though,
his back is straight, his tail is up
and he has brought his nose close
to her warm fleshy hands. His tongue,
or rather some dumb cells deep within
him know this flesh and want it

on his tongue. And she loves him.
She has brought her face close to his.
Her face is opened by what she feels
for this creature who has run to her
and brought her to this loving crouch.
In other parts of the painting is a path
these two could walk on, a stream, rocks
in the water they could walk on too,
a huge tree, a linden perhaps, a meadow,
sun-filled, where children are playing,
above them purple gashes in the land,
dark as omens, possible outcroppings
and suggestions of hills. At the top
of the scene is a small patch of sky.
It is blue, with some gray in it,
some green interestingly brushed in.
But down here, close and near are strong
and lean away from the cornered fugitive.

MY MOTHER TEACHES US TO SPEAK IN TONGUES

for Carmen Reiss

My mother believes in things that stay. Things
like silence-held she placed in shrines.
She would pray prayers without words in her bed
the whole night long. She trained our ears to listen
for that moment she would let the warmth
of words back in, take arms against silence,

write testimonials against it. She sang songs in shrines
against it, believed in the power of chanted novenas. Before bed-
time we had to kneel to prayer said out loud, listen
to expanded rosaries with "Hail, Holy Queens" in them; warmth
in our knees, embroidered prayers. Petitions against silence
were but one defense against unholiness in all things.

She heard the sacred in languages she did not know. In bed
she practiced Latin phrases she loved and listened
for at High Mass. She seemed to be in love with the warmth
of mouthing strange things. She bought Spanish records. Silence
became *silencio* on her thickened tongue. She believed in things
she liked the sound of: *no pue'o vivi'* and *labio de buiri* were shrines.*

We were fascinated with this new mother, listened
to her with new ears. She spiked her language with new warmth,
with lines from poems she memorized. Then she fell for silence
once again, took it on with exclusivity of illicit love. Things
we could not know about took her away to shrines
we could not enter. She bought navy sheets for all the beds

in the house. In late spring when light and warmth
returned, she would not come back. The tutelage of silence
held her through the daffodils blooming. All the things
she could have said had to be said in shrines
we built out of the habit of living with her. One bed
of new roses said something, eggplants another. We listened

to the bamboo popping in the grove. Flocks of nearly silent
birds patterned blank and tattered skies. Things
like the blue stone in her ring said something to us. Shrines
were built wherever we could build them. We turned beds
in parts of the garden we had never turned before, listened
for the holiness of emptiness like expectant penitents. *La chaleur*

on a fini par connaître une alliance d'affaires à toucher. Notre silence
était un silence enchâssé. On a appris à écouter
tout ce que la chaleur peut engendrer, tout ce que l'amour peut accoucher.‡

* *No pue'o vivi'* (I cannot live) and *labio de buiri* (too tired to speak) are
from "*Bruca Maniquá*," Arsenio Rodriguez, as recorded on *Buena Vista
Social Club Presents Ibrahim Ferrer.*
‡ "Warmth /we came to know in alliance of things to touch. Our silence
/was silence enshrined. We learned to listen /to whatever it is warmth
negotiates, whatever it is love embeds."
French translation by Barry Jean Ancelet.

II

Il y a des jours, mon petit chien,
c'est seulement un chien,
qu'une femme peut parler avec.

RELATIVES

first line from Karl Kirchwey's "Late Beauty"

The sounds of their names in my memory:
Philoman is a name filled with lilacs;
she is my grandmother.
Jean-Ba and Baboo are close to *Abba* and *Baba.*
Their little names make them our fathers.
Aristile and Aristide move in our histories like
Greek shields. Our family is filled with twins.
Odon, old guarded tongue,
my main and first father.
His koans were mostly in the language of silence.
Azalie is draped silk.
She is my great-grandmother's favorite sister.
Jan, as the Dutch pronounce it, as clean
and simple as a leaf.
At thirty his heart stopped.
Nips was my cousin. In church records
he is Napolean.
It was never clear if Nips was the best trickster
a village could ever have or just plain dimwitted.
It was never clear which was the better release,
to be inside his schemes or in the moment after.

EIGHT PRAYERS IN AN AUGUST GARDEN

for John Hathorn

1

The morning light.
The open ditch filled with equisetum,

2

the great snowy egret
in it.

3

A row of *Tithonia compositae*
burning like napalm,

4

that fire reflected in blue water.

5

Bright, hot noon
with cicadas,

6

their song
like Arab women
teaching their girl-children
grief.

7

Mid-afternoon sky
the color of dirt with lots of black in it,
a thousand storms inside.

8

The clearing after dark.

BONE FIRE

I am the ritual action, I the sacrifice, I the food-oblation,
I the fire-giving herb, the mantra, I the butter, I the flame,
and the offering too I am.
— "Works, Devotion, and Knowledge," *Bhagavad Gita*

for Parvathy Anantnarayan

My wife's new teacher is Indian.
He tells her first thing in the morning
to whirl like dervishes. When she stops,
he tells her to bring her hands together
before her face, to look at her thumbs
until the world stops spinning.
He tells her to do this three times.
Then there are five other things he says
she must do. She will grow old more slowly
doing this he tells her.

At the beginning of each day we try
to take darkness off our bodies.
Give ourselves naked to light.

Every year we pledge part of our mass
to whatever is larger than we are.

All summer we burn like the patchouli
in one neighbor's garden, the basil in another.

My friends Cindy and Luis have taken to
calling me Bubba. My nieces called me
Uncle Bubba before they called me any other
name. My sister calls me Bub when she wants
to be most endearing. There's something
in that name I should come to call holy,
as unimaginable as that might seem to me now.

I have never been thin. No one
in my family, on both sides, is thin
but I married a slim woman, loved her
nearly all my life now. Her mother is slim.
I once came relatively close to being slim.
My mother thought I was dying and told me so.

Winters my wife sleeps very close to me.
Says I am fire she needs. Her feet drift
toward me slowly, like gelid fish drifting
under ice.

I like to think of large thick roots
of the four o'clocks in our garden.
Mirabilis jalapa the scientists call these,
but this is a plant with no pretensions
to anything but small beauty, its flower
a small petalless spot, its emissary
quiet perfume for ground, wind, blue
in sky, even for the sharp silver air, latter
arrivant spinning in like holiness every year.

MAUNDY THURSDAY, PETER'S SONG

Thousands of years ago they say the prophet sat
with his disciples eating a spare last meal
in a dimly-lit room. Some were surely going to fat,

some lean, some ratty-haired, some slick as seals
in spite of the various ways the stories have tidied
up the scene. Artists later have them sit on deal

benches. Their robes are color matched, the mighty
one is always in the center, Judas on his left,
the other principal on the right. No one is flighty

in this narrative. The redbud tree bears a white heft
of flowers still. Peter does not feel himself a rock
of anything. He is hungry mostly, for fish, not bereft

or desolate — a loving, kindly man; not for tonight the shock
of his friends and his heart hanging in trees like ragged socks.

THINGS TO TEACH GRANDCHILDREN

    after Sei Shonagan

    for Dickie Wagner

Not to paint pictures for frames.
    The refrigerator door is an excellent place for a child's drawing.

How not to be afraid of rest.

Touching.

We are rooted to everyone in the family — the uncle who speaks louder
    and louder as he drinks; at the end of the day he is screaming
    everything to everyone. The aunt who is looking for the doctor
    who will finally know what is wrong with her. Our brother
    Chicken Little and his wife who must leave the party early.
    Our mothers who tell the same stories over and over again.

Heaven is an idea. It is attainable daily.

THREE POEMS FROM THE JAPANESE

1

Catfish in clear water
along the stretch of road
to my children's houses.
Wide blue ribbons waving
under bright duckweed.

2

The fog between the track
where quarter horses train
and the sun rises.
Memory persists
even as it is burned away.

3

Wet children
slip away quickly.
The muscles in the hand
grow slack and weak.
But the hand does not forget.

SCHUBERT AT BEETHOVEN'S FUNERAL

Ludwig van Beethoven, 1770–1827
Franz Schubert, 1797–1828

Beethoven on reading the songs from *Die Winterreise* on
his sick-bed: *Truly in Schubert there is a divine spark.*

Pallbearers all agree to it. Within and without they let themselves be dressed
in shade and gravity. When Schubert lighted his torch with the other mourners
he knew he was lighting a last light for all the old man loved. How incessance

of little things and the music lying in them
had always served him very well: the afternoon
silvering the brook with summer light, film
of anything once full and bright and strong, the moon

when it almost disappears, the way milk to skim
is tied to a young girl's song, death coming too soon,
music in the unoiled hinge, melody in the *hem-hem-*
hem of someone walking into the house, or toward loons.

Difficulty in this last act was not in remembering the way the deaf man obsessed
about almost everything. It was the old man as particular echo of every sojourner's
fate, to live so fully inside a plentitude of airs and then be of air finally dispossessed.

MY MOTHER'S MEMORY, PORTRAIT

With my mother it was always about not forgetting.
Early on she tied me to her. She was dedicated
to the physics and the flowers of memory.
My life under her tutelage would be a simple life.
Not forgetting the lines in the garden was my first lesson
in geometry even though I wouldn't know that for a long time.
Then there were other lessons of clear and clean effect.
Not forgetting to get to the road for the bus on school mornings.
Not forgetting that meals were for the construction of who we were
to be — not forgetting and just getting up and walking away
when one was full. Not forgetting to make my Easter Duties.
Not forgetting to visit my father's grave on the windy prairie.
Not forgetting to bring back only what was on the grocery list.
Remembering not to complain of the size of the bags I was given
to walk home with. She put nothing on the list she didn't have to have.
Remembering that a life cut away from past life is illusion.
Not forgetting to forge a life that was just my own.
To make us remember she used to send us back
to our houses with packs of frozen okra and sacks
of unhusked corn, with purple-hull peas and crates of potatoes,
with seven-steaks and pork roasts, with gumbos and jambalayas.
She tried her best to always be at the table if she could.
One day we remembered her in the peppers and the garlic,
one day in the shallots, in parsleys and green onion tops.
Another day it was flaked coconut in creamed icings,
or in little squares of chocolate as dark and sweet as fear.

TO BE OF USE

We would shed the long green coat
in the woods on cold bright days,
leave it there under bare trees
if we were called in suddenly.
We would forget about hair,
let it fall as it would, take on
smell of smoke in the clearing
and the cleaning of the woods.
To get caught in rainstorms,
to be covered with dust,
to sit for long sittings
so someone can see
how morning or winter light
or early evenings after sunset
color our flesh.
I know these things as the leaf
knows them.
To stand naked and weary
in the doorway next to lilac
bushes when we can tell ourselves
finally to break away for a time.
And then to go back to our stations,
our tongues silent in our heads.
To bend as we are directed to.
To become silk, hold beyond
a strength we know.
To be requisite to the act.
To spin like prayer.
To be part of the making.

DÜRER'S *APOLLO*

When Dürer drew Apollo, he placed him in a light-
er colored field surrounded by a golden
border. My friend Bill says it looks like a white kite,
this space the god stands in where he's shown holding
a happy sun. It is always morning here, flight
from morning some derivation of morning still; molten
noon, just morning terrified. We see what we might
call the lazy afternoon or advent of evening. Moldings
in our houses shift in dying light, a trick for our eyes
mostly. We even call dark *relief*, but Dürer was in love
with this god. He works the god's gold in hair that lies
on his manly shoulders in the portraits, in the gloves
of buttery yellow he gives himself to wear, in the ties
gleaming in his blouse and coat, in *Great Turf*, groves,
bees. Radiant prayer, world where morning never dies.

III

Et les Sainte-Marie
tout partout, mon frère.

THE BLUE BOAT

after Philip Gould's *Young Houma Indian Paints*
a Lafitte Skiff-Style Fishing Boat Near His House in Dulac

for Eric Turley

It was not as though he had to think of a special something
to get him. It was time for the child to have his boat.
This boy lived on water and in water, and he could lose
himself completely in some blue hinge-point where blue
of water and of sky mingled in each other on the horizon
where they met, a spot not unlike that spot in angel's wings

where flight's agency is joined. In his skiff-style fishing boat
he would make lines of those ineffable joints in the water, lose
himself momentarily like cartographers lose themselves in blue
of ocean and of rivers, in demarcations of verticals and horizon-
tals so that every terrestrial locus is held by conjunctions of wings.
Much we love we can't name, yet love holds itself out in something

or other we do name and cleave to. This boy's lesson is not about los-
ing more. He is already in love with liquefaction, transparent blue
he can disappear in. His father wants him to know that horizons
are ephemeral, places we go to and come home from, extended wings
we fly with to get us where we want to go; the wing but one thing
we travel by, the wind another, jumping off place another. This boat

he will himself lower into the water at Grand Caillou, into Bayou Blue
and Bayou Black. From this boat he will pick out anxious horizons
holding fishers who know the fierce wake of the Lafitte skiff, wings
of some avenging angel whose sweep and pull can change things
faster than anyone can be prepared for. To the spine of the boat
he fits his spine. In the necessity of drift he will attach himself to lose

only as much of himself as he lets himself lose. The stars from Orion's
Belt are his to pick from this reclination he learned from leaves. Wings
can fold in the nights on Des Allemands. On rundown docks something

as seemingly unflightworthy as the pelican folds on itself. One boat's
prow takes one gangly bird to rock for the night, then all boats lose
their boatness in birded dark. Sprouted sleepers take on a deeper blue

than all the blues around them. In the cypress trees and willows, wings
are turned in. In the Louisiana maples and the cottonwoods something
comes home to roost. Roseate spoonbills' nests high in trees are boats,
the web-footed sleepers on boats, boats; the drowsing boy, a boat he loses
in sleep and finds himself returned to in the morning. The glazed blue
he awakens into, then a shot-silk sky, expanse of lighted winged horizon,

a living, breathing something coming over the hull of his boat.
He could again lose himself for this red like his skin and sky blue
as love. He turns from the horizon; his own oars his own new wings.

BONNARD, *TRÈS PROFONDÉMENT AFFLIGÉ*

Bonnard was deeply distressed....
— Antoine Terrasse correspondence

Bonnard had this thing for edges,
for intriguing us with the parts
of things, with objects slipping
off the canvas almost, objects
almost evacuating the scene.
On these edges he registers
yet another degree of love in
and of the world. He habituates
affection inside these peripherals,
the very nearly absented snared
and clearly adored. For instance,
the young woman in the lower
right quadrant of *The Open Window.*
She is at rest, her head on blue cloth,
her eyes closed. In the painting
hardly anything else is at rest.
The trees lift themselves into
the blue pillow the sky is. They
strain against their rootedness.
Leafiness here is a song built
around a flush of blue notes.
The glass in the shutter, broken
reds and yellows, grays, blues
of the pillow sky and the rocker
pillow. The striped wallpaper
is a breathtakingly simple line
in some melody in a jazz dream
someone is having. We can see
the upper reaches of heaven
through a reed shade. Bonnard
does things like that — giving
heaven an awning. He so loves
the world he translates the other-

worldliness heaven might be,
brokers a heaven that is here
and not lessened by being here.
Under this heaven and next to
a woman whose closed her eyes,
the lover-painter has painted
her little pet; he has painted it
so loosely it might be mistaken
for Marthe's dog. But for us
who know Marthe and expect
her to show up often in these scenes,
we are instructed otherwise.
Bonnard is watching Renée
Monchaty. The little animal
is watching him watching her.
We are watching a whole system
of exchange. She is his lover
here in Dauberville. She addresses
her postcards to him to Marthe too,
will kill herself in a hotel in Paris
in three years. But in this room
in 'Ma Roulotte' he places her
hand on the chairback, lets her
touch her little friend. The year
is 1921. The man just outside
the scene lives inside his paints
and inside recent wars. A woman
he cannot help but love is here.
She gives herself to him again
this afternoon, her drowsing head
a vegetative rhyme for trees
above her. Open windows open
everywhere on one archaic smile —
ancient sign of pleasure given,
taken-pleasure's ordinary register.

FAINT SPECKS IN WHISTLER'S NOCTURNES

After we have turned dryness over in our hands, we wet
our fingers to keep turning pages. Repeatedly offered dark
is something we can begin to see inside of. Silent
children draw us, invite investigation of what is asleep
or awake inside them. What is outwardly unconcerned
often concerns us most.

The way Whistler, for instance, was so in love with dark
grays and browns. The way even his explosions, silenced
in his nocturnes, do not silence the nocturne itself. Asleep
in farthest depths of his fathomless nights is the unconcerned,
faint speck, of blue, red, or yellow — jewel almost,
but paint really, just that, glistening, after years seemingly wet

still. Inside one of these specks you could reside, be more silent
than you've ever been, but not a place you are dumbly asleep.
This place, if we can call it that, is for that unconcern
that forgets tasks — who to call, what is needed most
for supper tonight, whether we have left the clothes wet
in the washer. In this room of sorts is the dark

lover who will lull you into a sleep
you have seldom, if ever, known. The lover here is unconcerned
with what you want to garden, sew, cook, what you need to see most
clearly. This lover will not let you plead the perspiring wet
fever brings. You will think the burden is another older darkness
you have always dragged around with you. The silent

configurations outside your window are necessarily unconcerned.
You want those apparitions to be trees mostly,
but anything that moves would do. Wings making flapping wet
sounds would be a song, a falling light in the dark,
twelve shepherds singing of a night holy and silent,
you and they drifting off into the hymn, into sleep.

This drift is what you know now you have needed most.
In this moment you will consecrate your holiest wet
rites. You will be taken to a river glassed darkly
to keep you from consumptive light. Silences
will lie upon you in layers in this sanctified sleep
and you will waken momentarily into this blessed unconcern.

ROSA PARKS ANGEL

> *. . . it's not just what she did, but God's use of her in the*
> *fullness of time. There's something divine about her.*
> — Rev. Jessie Jackson, *Cincinnati Enquirer*

We do not know which hands first cupped her
head and then her backside, perhaps a midwife
her mother knew, and her mother's mother;

someone familiar expecting her, the new life
attached to everything around it. Her father,
the carpenter, would have provided the knife

or something sharp to cut into this world a way
for her; then lessons in attachment, how one room
grows another room until it is a house, how sway
reduces itself in acts of adding. Loose space looms

precariously, then seeks rectitude. On that day
she made a new world in her sitting, domes of some
heavens shook. Only the weak domes, she might say,
like straw feathers in angels' wings or wayward brooms.

LIGHT AT THE EDGE OF THE WETLANDS

for Victoria Turley

These two are bent close to the ground,
study the fold of some surface minutia
introducing itself into whatever they are doing here.
The slight girl-child, this squat, grave man
who must be her grandfather, are situated near
a little yellow boat on the strip of sand
between the water and this other sea of marsh grasses.
They will be pulled apart, have other thirsts
to slake. All that will come later though.
Now, in this light they seem as calm
as machinery idling, as insistently present
as the locusts in the chênières singing
of song and of time, without knowledge of either.
Locust songs go on until they simply stop.
Theirs might be one of the songs of perfected being,
as is beatification in *V*s of light on water,
a water dance of seeming progression to the shore
and then the regressive dance back to the horizon
as if light itself were in search of rhyme.
What hunger or what thirst the pelicans know here
is pelican hunger and pelican thirst.
The low sky rests like a heavy silver knife
on this dark water. Above, the sky is blue
of sky over water on clear fall days
everywhere. And this man and this child,
the yellow boat shines on them like a lantern
placed on the ground to shine on them.
These are the incarnations of dumb thirst
the saintly pray for incessantly,
thirst that we might even call knowledge
if knowledge can be accounted for
by something that has everything to do
with not knowing.
This is the dumb thirst canvases have for wet paint.
This is the holy thirst drawing us to the water's edge.

JEAN MARAIS' NIGHT OUT

Jean Marais, 1913–98

Behind the lace curtains
Dinah Washington sings.
The stones in the streets
lined with plane trees
coax music out of the dark
sounds an approaching figure
makes. Her shoes raise her
above her ordinary height.
In the café one man whispers
in another's ear. The old man
presides over money and prayer
beads from his seat near
the register. Tonight a brawl
will ensue. Death will come
awfully close to someone here.
A woman with severely made up
eyes will smoke long white
American cigarettes and speak
to no one all night long.
The white handkerchief
with embroidered edges
will wipe blood seeping
slowly from a nose or mouth.
Someone will be offered another
chance, but much will not turn
out right. Someone will find
the ragtime cds finally,
will hand them to the sound man.
He will play them until daylight.
Then they will come for the body.

VAN GOGH COMES TO LOUISIANA *LE JOUR DE LA TOUSSAINT*

The enduring ache brought on again.
His three small boats still shimmer
in the mudflats at the edge of the water.

Van Gogh falls through the sky and begins
his inquisition along this distant water splintered
by sunlight. He has found another luminescence

he can love as he loves the god in his paints.
I can hear the flat, Dutch-Frenchness in his voice
in the letter he writes to his brother,

"There is not one light here better than another.
The light in the pines in the forest,
the light fused in reeds along lakes and bogs.

Amsterdam is everywhere.
Abbeville is Auver-sur-Oise in this light.
Here the Camargue is Holly Beach and Cameron,

Kaplan and Gueydan.
And, here and there, little boats
overturned sometimes, their hulls red, yellow,

green, blue like paints straight from the tubes.
In the rice fields green like willows
in Japanese prints,

like *céladon* in late evening
and early morning.
Et les Sainte-Marie tout partout, mon frère."

LOUISIANA MAPLES IN LATE WINTER

for Tim Gautreaux

In that time before we can rightly call anything spring,
they show themselves. They bear the year's first color
and they call us to them. Later clear translucence will
seep into the green in our cypresses. Our newly green
oaks will block the sky with gold. Silver will cling
to the undersides of everything pushing toward growth,
and bamboo in the groves will snap their thin sheaths
at joints in the canes. The percussives will be day-long,
little offices or holy music in our gardens until dusk
cools them down. The rest of the woods will remain
utterance of winter still, a spare and sharp calligraphy
of all mostly mute, the sometime sullen underneath
of things. But in early February *Aceraceae rubrum*
claims its own key. From high pale peach to ranges
of claret and garnet they line our roadsides, nascent
blossoms propellered rhymes, the lively quick of fires
of missiles from other worlds with new poems in them.

QUARTET, WITH REMBRANDT

Neither human beings nor string quartets possess fixed
meanings.
— Joseph Horowitz on Shostakovich, *New York Times*,
February 6, 2000

The music critic speaks of Shostakovich when he says that
humans and quartets do not possess fixedness, but must let go
the way Manet, perhaps, might let his figures go in small flat-
bottomed boats, a boy against shimmering river water ever about to row.

Beauty in Vermeer is always beauty unhinged. Look at his *Girl with a Red Hat.*
Beauty herself, she enlarges beauty her creator would come to know
in her kin. In her startled mouth under the red brim, the catch
is the catch of unguarded grace. We see it again in the snow

of a pearl swinging near the face of the blue-turbaned girl
and in the milk forever falling from the milkmaid's jar.
In Rembrandt's self-portraits in old age we see the curl

almost gone from his large full-bodied head. He would not mar
a life he was glad to have had. That life had unfurled
like music. It held on to nothing in the end, nothing near, or far.

WHAT'S REALLY GOING ON IN *A DUTCH COURTYARD*: THREE ADULTS WITH CHILD WITNESS

A Dutch Courtyard
Pieter de Hooch, 1629–1683

What these people have withdrawn from is large.
Immeasurable is what they have been drawn toward.
A whole town with churches and a marketplace, barges
in the waterways near the loading docks, the guard
drowsing near the banking house with gleaming sword
lie in the precincts just beyond their wall. A red serge
she's opted for is but one bright, desired thing; a word
in private, full tankards, exchangeable heat. Courage
is what it takes to cash in toil for velvets and leather,
or to catch the beauty of a man's limb and not flinch;
in the lifted glass she tells them afternoons in the heather
field is a possibility if they play their cards right. Wench
is a laughable appellation in this close company. Whether
or not ships sail, a possibility. Glee in moorings, a cinch.

VISION OF AUGUSTIN NOVICE

From detail of *The Death of St. Francis*,
Ambrogio Bondone Giotto, 1267?–1337

He can hardly take it in, this boy monk
we see transfixed in the plaster at Santa Croce.
He does not see anything anymore
of the celery-colored walls enclosing him
in the large room in the monastery
where they've allowed the youngsters in
for witnessing. The older monks have gathered too
to see their brother Francis draw his final breath.
This is something they should see, the old men say,
this final shedding after all an echo of that time
in the piazza when the youngster shed his silk robe
and its ties before his father and his father's friends,
a silk robe not unlike the pale green drape here pulled
back to frame the detail by a tentative inquiring hand,
the little hand translucent, as finely-boned as bird wing.
This boy had mostly lost his way in the world
and he stands here much as the boy saint stood
before his startled father and the other merchants
drawn from negotiations in their shops and stalls.
The little monk had just as well be disrobed too.
All sentience in him has fallen from him.
Look at the way his mouth falls open, dumb holiness.
Look at the glazed astonished eyes, at the way he leans
into the lift like a leaf lifted in the windy currents
between the cloister well and the cloister wall.

THE JAX BEER SOFTBALL TEAM

My father is the one with the faintest smile,
the one kneeling on the first row, third from left.
Their tongues are parched now but within minutes
they will all regather in the pool hall. They will play
for hours in the lilac neon, kindly ancillary night
to counter each bulb burning over tables like a last leaf
on winter trees. Their silk jackets lie in piles
on chairs near the door. These men have put in more miles
than they care to remember. The few chances my father leaves
on the table make him legend here, as does the lightest
way he hangs suspended in his signature slide. Trays
of their sponsor brew sustain the after-spin. Remnants
of the game keep them happy here. A slap, a pat, the heft
and drag of things outside the game delayed for just a while.

MY MOTHER GETS DRESSED FOR SUNDAY MASS

My mother didn't know Oscar Wilde,
would have thought him ridiculous
for saying something like "Appearance
is everything." She was no decadent,
could not, even with studied effort,
have entertained the idea. She believed
in a literal heaven where she would again
touch loved ones who had gone there
before her, be with them for the happiness
eternal those long Louisiana afternoons
had prepared her for. Looking good
was a given there, and she was going
to look good here doing this church-going
thing she'd always done, and this looking
good often began and ended with a small
round box of Coty. While we waited
restlessly for her in the car in the driveway
she would do one last check in the glass.
She took the box decorated with powder-
puffs looking like the very art-nouveau fans
Wilde and his lascivious friends might
have fanned themselves with (but none
of these tropes really touched her,
she didn't even know art-nouveau,
or its love of Egyptian classicism,
or belle-époch, or any of that stuff,
and had she known these things, would
gladly have sent them all to the hell
they worked so hard to get into.)
What she did do was to pull the skin
on her nose down by tightening the muscles
of her upper lip. She would tone and reduce
sheen there first. Then she would veil
the rouge on her high cheekbones.
Planes above her eyebrows she muted.
Then finally she lifted her chin,

swathed her neck to within a hairline
of the cutwork lapels of her blue serge
suit, and just when we thought for sure
she had rooted herself before that mirror,
she fixed with amazing quickness
the straw pillbox and was in the car.
She always looked the way she wanted
to look. And what she did was right
and just. No acing off — more a song
of praise. What lord would have wanted
less from one of his beloved after all.

MARY IN *THE SMALL CRUCIFIXION*

a meditation after Grünewald

It had all begun much earlier.
One is not crucified in an hour or a season.
Even Peter knew beforehand he would be the one
to drive in the first nail so to speak.
By the time the cock had sounded his first full note
everything they prayed with would unravel.
But even before that Mary couldn't breathe.
It was most like that other moment
when she was told what was inside her then.
The angel with immaculate wings had put something
sounding like some large salvation before her.
But as she knelt before him, or he before her
—the image makers vary on this point—
she felt her life splintered from within.
In his prayer to her, her glory was to carry this thing
inside her and then to let it go. In his prayer
she was to be a husk holding holiness tenderly.
She knew when angels come with announcements
nothing could ever make things simply otherwise.
She knew too what birth engenders finally.
She would have to give her assigned miracle away
again and again, the giving ever larger every time.
Some icon makers have her holding her hand up
to the messenger in this annunciatory scene.
Some see in the raised hand a sign of gestural grace.
Some see in the raised hand a prayer of sacral doubt.

FISHING OFF BELLE ISLE

for Andrew Reiss

On some Good Friday afternoons it seemed our population split.
Some good people could not withstand the lures of the office of worship.
The stations of the cross. The other services from noon to three.
The delicious denial of heartbreakingly beautiful spring.
The occasional spring storm driving us inside.
The purple silk covering all the iconography in the church.
The empty monstrance on the altar.
The opened door of the tabernacle, the black square the open door makes.
Admonitions against work in the garden.
The wooden clacker the boy called the penitents with.
The antiphonal click of beads on church pews.
Old women in long black dresses.
Their plain black hats, their *tignons*, and lace head-coverings.
The old men with white brows near hairlines.
The slight young quarter horse rider and the blacksmith.
Children mostly cleansed of confutation mixed into the lines of confessors.
But spiritual fibrillation possible on or near water is another kind of call.
On the little plank projections over the water at False River
near the last vestiges of quarter life on Parlange, two boys take worms
they dug up yesterday and they fish.
Reese Spooner has just sprinkled parsley seed on a bed he prepared
yesterday.
He lets a burlap sack fall on the seeded area.
He only slightly moves the soil as he gathers the sack up again.
This is not digging in the soil on the holy day.
At some point a burlap sack will fall out of a busy man's hands
when he has fishing on his mind,
and he will have to pick it up and the soil may move just a bit
as he moves, but he does not move soil.
My friend Brenda and her husband leave early.
They will fish south of Delcambre.
My grandson Andrew is a serious, shy and loving boy.
He is asking his father to take him to the camp below Dulac.
He wants his cousin William to come too.

And Victoria and Carmen, and Jamie and Eric, and his Uncle John.
On Highway 20 between Chacahoula and Schriever old men
and old women sit on plastic buckets. They fish in water running
like a wide ribbon the whole length of the road.
In expanded waters near Des Allemands women and children
cross as they move among long, quiet fishing geographies.
They drift, wave to each other.
In pockets throughout the Atchafalaya Basin fishers dot surfaces,
or they shimmer in the ether just above.
In water everywhere fish sense is divination atomistically construed.
Now in the worm, now in the holy boy who is my grandson.
In the trucker and the welder and their wives.
In the clerk and in the retired bishop drowsing in his large chair.
And in fishes moving toward fishes swimming in dreams.

WYETH AND HELGA IN *AUTUMN*

The sun can still burn fiercely in these declensions
of light this time of year. In this sun he places her
near an ancient tree about to lose whatever sums
of leaves it barely holds on to. Light he scatters
variously and perhaps he makes us want to think
this is as much a painting about light as anything.
He plays with light in and on branches, on brinks
of inclinations, in lilac-lighted overtones, in rings
of fiery orange some blurred tree or hillside makes,
in the buttery yellow of a quickly cooling sky, blue
barely hinted at, hardly blue at all. It is how he takes
away argument for one thing or another that is news
here. She is sun loved by sun. The old sun spent rake,
beggar for play on face and hair, a gospel with a muse.

POSTCARD FROM CHINA

for Li-Young Lee

He writes "the man on the card
is either you or me in a previous life."
The wind at the man's back displaces
cherry blossoms, blows them past him.
The sash holding his white robe
blows away from him too, red crescent
made to rhyme with the thinning moon
in the far reaches of a vast blue heaven.
O.K., I will let this pale suspension,
poet, or sage, or both, be me, drowsy
extension of some dreaming axiom-
maker making axioms as observable
workings inside an inflectioned world.
Even though he looks more like Lee,
I am rising to wherever I am going.
There is no hard evidence of anything
touching anything in the spare report.
The rendered moon loves the man
but the two will be ever untoward.
The colophon looks like tangled red
roots unattached to anything. (Leaves
coming in after the flowers, fruit
coming after leaves are wherever they
are before they are leaves and fruit
and they are absented in this scene.)
It is a painting about wind and drift
which my friend sees me as figure in.
I am happy to be there. I am happy
my friend sees me in confluences
and in contingencies which he says
might include the deaths of fathers,
the vacuity of air without them in it;
in persimmon trees we might plant
to give them a place in this garden
the world is, or persimmon or wind

poems we write when fathers press
themselves beyond dreamless days
toward the blowy present memory is.

THE PHOTOGRAPH

We are drawn to this calligraphy
of light just as we are drawn
to light itself. We waken to light
entering rooms we are asleep in.
Years after photons draw us
into the inebriations we call life,
work, love, and the requisite
pauses we predictably pose for,
we seek what we have stored away.

Take this one, for instance, of my grandfather.
One aunt posits he has just come from his green fields,
just bathed, just put on those seersucker slacks,
that starched white shirt, just lighted
the Picayune between his fingers whose plume
of smoke rises into the sheer curtain blown toward him.
The other woman in this scene presents another case.
Just look, my mother says, at that swollen face.
That gazing into distance is insatiable thirst.
He will, she says, get up in a minute
and walk into town. Even rain would not keep him
when he gets like this. He may be gone for days.
He will have to be brought home by his wobbly friends.
They will all lead wobbly lives.
He will teach them shame and fear.

Whatever adjudications there are here, they are theirs —
He will not move like light in grasses moves.
He does not stir like dust in sudden summer rains.
He has never been a green thought in a green world,
is indifferent to these flashes every time they dig him up.

JACOB'S ANGEL

Early in the evening Jacob is alone. Everything is so quiet
he thinks he can hear the water moving between the riverbanks.

Heat leaves the land quickly here but falling asleep had fallen
upon him as tenderly as a light kiss. But then something tearing

him brought water to his eyes. Light or flesh he could not see
held him in this too closedness he knew would stop his breath.

This angel, if we can call it that, would make him cry out
and then it would let him go. It would watch, it seemed,

for the breathing to slacken to normalcy and then come for him
again and again. That is until Jacob, old grabber of heels,

would finally fight the fight so truly the angel would be forced
to beg for leave. Jacob thinks he may have died that night,

reminds himself the muscled dream surely faded in the morning
light. But what is he to make of this new body in the broad field

he has been told is his new name? And what is this fierce
angelism he feels behind him rustling his blouse, moving slowly

through the hairs on the back of his head? *Oh, fierce friend,*
I limp like a prayer, cannot breathe at all without you now.

STAY

All those days stretching into weeks the blossoms' buds swell.
They stay contained in lilac-chilled and nascent air then burst
in their own time like the sexy things they are. To clearly tell
what gives the greater pleasure we can barely know. Our first

spinning toward the cliff's edge and that moment just after
we lose contact with matter does pitifully little to help us.
When do we know what silk feels like, or ice, or laughter?
When we hold what we call silk, or stay near cold with just

the right mind of silk or ice? What to hang on those trotlines
translating joy? Wherever cast, lines resist and refuse to stay
in belly, heart, or near the tongue. We say *soul* perhaps, find
on landing there as leafy and pied a slope as anywhere. Say

whatever we want to say, lilacs flowering are like kids in birches,
their joys are on all the branches, in staying still and in the lurches.

BACH'S LAST SURGERY

In those last days when he could see nothing,
he kept seeing the blue plate in the kitchen
against the white wall on the shelf high above
and about six phrases away from the fire
in the grate. In this plate pink steaming pears
were brought to his table, white flesh of fish,
sausages piled high to falling, and grapes
like small green mountains filled with song.
In this latter darkness some moments came to him
like walls he found himself standing too close to.
Here he could see nothing but the blankness
of the mass, blocked delineation and demarcation
blurred, so much loss for him in this heavy lack
of light. In this kind of night all could crumble,
whole buildings, the rooms he had lived in
all his life, architectures his own hands realized,
taken down by wrecking crews. In those moments
he was saved by the plate. It was the blue ecstasy
he carried in him after a day's work. He took it
to Barbara's bed and then to Anna Magdelena's bed.
It was the moon the night he came home to absence
too large to breathe in. His friends had met him
at his door. She could not be kept any longer,
they told him. Then they took him to the kitchen
where he sat under the blue hanging there like a light
in his grief thinking of her strong arms, strong legs,
her strong faith that even his sometimes paled next to,
this music in a woman God had given him and had taken
away. This plate was the blue disk the sun turned into
above that rocky eastern hill so far away, that holy land
he would never travel to, all this business, so much work
to do here. That plate, and then this music clearly
hearable now in each attendant child still alive,
in attendant wife or attendant nurse approaching his bed.
The variant music in the shutters being opened
to the clear air of midyear in this high elevation

he was dying in. A phrase a knitting needle falling
on the tiles in the next room makes, and the last music
in the falling, him reaching for something he thinks
at first might be paper before he knows that it is not.
His writing hand, if he could see it, would surely still
be stained, as it always was. The needle's phrase inverts
itself. It is the song in the wall between his room
and the adjacent room it fell in. The phrase wants
something else to happen to it as it always did.
As it always did, the last phrase the needle made,
and it was enough for him in that final hour or so.

NEWLYWEDS NEAR HIGH ISLAND, AUGUST 29, 1937

for Joseph Valerie and Gladys Wimberly Bourque

Somewhere between Sabine Pass and High Island they stop
to stretch their legs. They have left large families
in the prairie turning to farmland at the edges
of the wetlands they call home. In the distance behind
them there are no wading birds skittering and hopping
from one sand-burrowed creature to another. No entreaties
of wind, or heat, or bright light. Neither copses nor sedges
vie for anything in their world. These youngsters are blinded
in this calm moment. The breakers barely break. Copulatives
here are object rhymes. His straw hat, held to suggest ease,
is angled toward her straw bag. His left arm a wedge
just barely touching her right shoulder. They are still finding
their way toward each other. They've just begun to unravel
long enduring love, are new to stoppage in extended travel.

JIZO'S FROG AND THE LILACS IN MARQUETTE

The old poet putting a frog in Jizo's lap
puts a frog in your lap, and saintliness too
if you make your lap a resting space. That lilac
hedge is no dividing line. I planted it hoping you
loved lilacs and would stop one day to take
some. You'd be rushing home, nothing could be new
again in your world. But here you are breaking
armloads of these bluesful tongues. Your bike
lies on the side of the road. Reach and stretch you make
congruent to a silken act. After this, what, you say. Pike,
rabbits, doves! A new leaf turns and you will not know
the when and how of it. You count on things: a strike
of lightning in only one place, your horse to win the race,
the spin of risky tastes. Why too not saintliness and grace?

THE OWL IN VITA SACKVILLE-WEST'S GARDEN

Of those evenings lilac never completely leaves
the night sky, her son Nigel likes to tell
of a rare spin still of a white owl under the eaves
crowded with noisettes and bourbons, of the swell
of a full moon's light on the spathed silk
of Arum lilies with their bright yellow tongues, and smells
rising from pale ground flowers. If his mother found Bells
of Ireland pale enough or if leaf could approximate milk,
he recounts, it was considered for a bed. Workers felled
any bud turning purple or red. She wanted each night to weave
as this one kind of night could weave, an illuminated spell
cast by dark, dirt, muck and air: the flowering mind. To cleave
to such was a first lesson she learned and perhaps the last.
Roses school us so and the owl too every time he makes his pass.

MY FATHER IN THE SUN

When I first see him, he is sitting on the back steps
of the house we live in. He has taken off his shirt,
rolled the bottoms of his khaki pants. He has left
his shoes and socks inside and we have never seen
him outside without them on. He is a proper, shy
man, would not consider disrobing more than this.
I know it is September because the spider lilies
my mother planted are blooming in the beds
on either side of the door that serves as a backdrop
to this scene. He is a different father from the one
who wore a cap and long-sleeved shirts to pick
figs before the heat of the July day really set in.
This is a different father from the one who works
long hours without complaint. This is one scene
we will not see repeated. He has given himself over
to the luxury of sun for simple pleasure. He has
even oiled his skin, closed his eyes as he rests
his head on the door itself, opened the insides
of his white arms while the darker sides barely
touch his upraised knees. He was stationed briefly
in California in the war and then he came home
to us. He went every summer to some coastal town
or another with his mother when he was a child.
I'd like to think he is close to water in this scene.
I'd like to think he dreamed a heaven he could go to.

From *Call and Response: Conversations in Verse*

with Jack B. Bedell

2009

DÜRER'S MEDITATION ON SMALL THINGS:
THE GREAT PIECE OF TURF, 1503

It is the composition I am forever walking by
moves me most when I finally stop to look.
What is it turning us outside ourselves, what hook
hooks us and pulls us from whatever sky

we have come to inhabit as though we love
there and only there? It is a switch
after all, this hook. It shifts horizons. Heavy mauve

the sky can be is eclipsed by something as neatly stitched
as this little patch of earth. I have measured what moved
me here, this patch is small by any standard but so rich

we could get lost in this country of green if we were to try.
A small golden ribbon of a snake, you ask. It is your book
to read. Crested dandelion stems, landscapes of crooked
grasses. What my eye loved I made for your eye.

LETTER FROM LEBANON

first line from Aga Shahid Ali's "Homage to Faiz Ahmed Faiz"

for Faraj Farajalla

You wrote this from Beirut, two years before
you finally left for good. You said your losses
were almost more than you could bear, scores
of friends had to flee, aunts and uncles tossed

like trees in a storm that never let up. Waving
goodbye was as incessant as waves in the sea
you played in as a child. The moon's paving

a road in water, the only road you could be
on in those nights. You had to take what they gave.
You had to pretend to like it until you could freeze

your heart. Bombs shattered and shifted more
than stores and houses. In churches crosses
toppled and fell. Blood, gasoline, and hatred poured.
Gardeners torched roses, cedars, scorched the mosses.

SCRATCH

Since that afternoon years ago
when my mother put us on our knees
and told us she was leaving,
I have placed myself in the world,
measured myself against the horizon,
let the sky cover me like some angel bird
hovering. I have seen wide ribbons
of pine making a trot-line at the earth's edge.
I have studied things up-close: stunted trees
growing out of rock. I have gone beyond
tree lines where grasses open seedpods
like prayers. I have stood at the water's
edge and wobbled, and still no one
knows who knifed the unreadable lettering
on my mother's new cedar chifferobe
that day. She and my father drove to town
to buy garfish for our usual Friday supper
at my aunt's house. We were questioned again
on her return but no one confessed — through
the fish cleaning, the seasoning, the frying.
I can't remember when exactly we laughed
and ran through the yard with our cousins.
It was night when we went home. We were happy.
Just last week, some fifty years later,
one of us brings it up in my mother's
presence. She has not walked for years
and it is no big matter to her now,
but none of us are fessing up today either.
We all know who didn't do it,
and one of us knows who did.

QUIETISM

first line from Naomi Shihab Nye's
"Walking Down Blanco Road at Midnight"

It happens in a quiet place.
If too much is moving around,
you never get to see the thin line
of red flickering above the horizon
just before sunrises or just after
sunset — some tag of fire or herald
of no sound whatsoever.
There is a moment when all leave
the table but something still breathes
as fat congeals on plates left behind.
The big chair in the yard near the oak
lived in the silence of trees in forests.
The tools put up in the winter shed,
silent in their work and in their rest.
An audiologist's finest instrument
might never record the calla lily's
slow, long, unfolding song.

LOVESICK: FROM LESBOS TO NASHVILLE

The moon just went behind a cloud
To hide its face and cry
from "I'm So Lonesome I Could Cry"
The Hank Williams' Songbook

Sappho, trans (in italics) by Mary Barnard

(*§ 37 You know the place: then*)

I prayed you would
come to me. I tried
to lure you with murmuring
of streams in stands
of apple trees.
You were with someone else
you could not leave.
Bees made music for you
in your own lemon grove
in Crete.

219

(§ 39 *He is more than a hero*)

I tried and tried to tell you
how I could not speak
if I met you suddenly.
I tried to move you, even
with a broken tongue.
A thin flame, I told you then,
runs under my skin.
Well, today blood
could hardly be said to run.
A wafting of ashes
there instead; sick birds
struggling in the lightest
winds.

(§ 42 *I have not heard one word from her*)

All that talk about unwilling
parting, all that poetry
about our gifts to Aphrodite,
how you melted me
in that sad hour
with sung apologies.
You could not leave,
you said, without reminding
me *"no voices chanted*
choruses without ours,
no woodlot bloomed in spring with-
out song . . ."
I hung on your every word,
asked you only to remember
who you left hobbled.
It is no wonder
the moon just went behind a cloud
to hide its face and cry.

(§ 45 *If you will come*)

I shall put out
new [skin] *for*
you to rest on

(§ 63 *Last night*)

I dreamed [...]
You and I had
words: Cyprian

My skin crawled —

(§ 87 *We know this much*)

Death is an evil;
we have the gods'
word for it; they too
would die if death
were a good thing

When you left,
it was like death.

Birds of ash
in the lemon
grove had no song.
They were not nightingales,
did not know what to do
in a world unlighted.
The hours could
weigh heavily,
or could not.
It was nothing to them.
Someone slipped the knot
of gravity.

It was like death.
We know this much.

THE ARUM LILIES IN MY MOTHER'S DREAM

My mother says he looks like he just stepped out
of a photograph in this visitation. This man, my father,
is wearing a blue seersucker suit and a red tie.

This is the man who never wore a blue anything
and he never owned a red tie. But he is here
in her dream. He barely speaks in this apparition.

He pushes his chair from the table, gets up
and stands for a moment seeming to admire
the arum lilies she's brought in from the garden.

She could not have told if he had any feeling at all
for flowers. He seldom said what he liked. A moment
only, then these flowers, and then he says he has to go.

EGRET HAIKU

1

Rising from grasses,
egrets in the farthest field,
spume on a green wave.

Egrets in rice fields,
I sew this year's kimono —
spring flight in green silk.

2

Egrets follow close
to my tractor in the field —
they love grubs I turn.

In midsummer light
we hardly see the egrets —
white enlightenment.

3

A flock of egrets
turn sharply back to the earth —
love turns on itself.

Egrets on branches
in trees in the rookeries,
white autumn tree lace.

4

In winter ditches
egrets and equisetum —
yellow and green sprouts.

Whole flocks of egrets
stitched into a large, thick quilt —
I dream white bird dreams.

ON AN OVERGROWN PATH

after Leoš Janáček

for Karen

The red table still holds its redness
after all these years. It is chairless
now, this table we took our meals on.
But the lilies you planted in the borders
still bloom every month as you planned
it. Spider lilies in September, arum lilies
throughout the summer, amaryllis in
the early spring and crocuses and tulips
and hyacinths in their time. Nun's
orchids are still here among the weeds
and grasses as is the evergreen wisteria
with Zéphirine Drouhin roses twining
through it, dropping petals in our plates.
And we are here too, surveyors upright
and open, in the tangle we still tend.

HOLLY BEACH, 1952

I was ten when my parents brought me to the beach for the first time,
and it was somewhat hard to tell what of this greyish brown was sand
and what was water. There was clearly something happening in the line
where the horizon was supposed to be, some curve I knew from land

and how it met the sky. I was not completely unfamiliar with rhymes
the earth itself teaches the young who look and measure, with strands
that finally knit themselves into some kind of rope of meaning, fine
distinctions that merge into larger being. But I had never had to stand

by myself before something I could walk into like this, could climb
into, it seemed to me, as the gulf shaped itself into this bulge, a grand
stilled opacity that did not even look like water. I had surely primed
myself to bravery as parents and aunts and cousins and sisters fanned

behind me in their own play. But when the water finally surged around me,
I was ten, could never have imagined such rotary or how to hold a dizzy sea.

EINSTEIN'S VIOLIN

He lived in a world where things fell short,
and it was in that very world where he enlarged
everything we knew about its ways. His heart
would not abide lockstep of any kind. Charged

orders for him were thoughts so wild and untamed
the maths to chart them often wouldn't follow. He failed
at marriages and loves; one beloved son he named

Tete fell into holes that swallowed him. But he sailed
in hard times wherever he could find water, framed
grief and loss with yet another leap he shaped and nailed

into a poetry of physics — straight lines curve *en fin*, part
of a way to explain a universe no one could have carved
before him. Always by his side the violin, Bach & Mozart
to visit with: sound, a bright smile; memory, a line curved.

DÜRER'S *POND IN THE WOODS*

In Dürer's brush no one is surprised by loss
or plenty. The trees on the left are but shafts
of what they once were. Under them mosses
spill through rocks and grasses. He's drafted

a little beach on the other side. A white
triangle at the foot of a stand of fir
or some other conifer. Here, one might

imagine lovers emerging or saints stirred
by waves of passion. Here, the inky night
suggested by dark water & clouds perturbed

in a golden sky are but another jostling
of light and dark, an allegory he's crafted
in paint. Everywhere there is murk and dross.
Everywhere there is to everything light grafted.

THE HAND OF THOUGHT

We have this notion about the roads we walk
on. We think that if we should cross a bridge
once, it will be there to cross again. We stalk
regularity and sameness; we want the ridge

we covered yesterday to be the one seam
we can rely on forever. We want the window's
in our houses to give us steady beams

of light. In autumn we want yellow indoor
light to fall softly on the carpets, the creams
and reds and blues hardly disturbed. Winter

light will be dense and heavy, table weight. Talk,
but nothing to do us in. Something in us cringes
at the thought of running into things and we bark
at anything — boulders, leaves, swarms of midges.

ON LISTENING TO SCHUBERT

It is mechanics of mind
that intrigues me most
in Schubert's Quintet, Opus 163,
all that initial creeping
necessary
for what is being
set up.
Grief underlies all
it tries to cover up.
In this geography, it matters
little if the sky is blue
with mares tails
or blue without,
if the sky
is the hot white
the sky becomes at noon
on clear summer days,
or a veiled
white sky
with thinly falling
snow.
Or slate,
or black with thunderheads,
or not.
We are mostly moved away
and not toward
anything,
the strings
our only
consolation.

PHOTOGRAPH FOR MY FATHER, 1944

In this one photograph of my mother
with her first three children, I am three.
My father is in California. My mother
is beautiful in this new role she's in.
My older sister looks directly at the camera.
Her beauty is straight-ahead beauty.
My younger sister turns her face
to the side, her beauty devastatingly oblique,

then and now. I am blank-faced with loss.
We are all being shaped by the very gift
we are trying to get to him before he's shipped
out. He will fade differently for each of us.
He will come home. He will tend to us
in his quiet way. Each of us will go on.
I will put lilies on his grave at Eastertime.

FRIDAY NIGHT FISH FRY

We have all gathered under the oak tree
in the back yard. The fish is frying
in one black pot, and over on the other fire
is my aunt's courtboullion made from three
large catfish the men caught earlier in the day.
It is not dark yet, but the moon in the east
is a large yellow plate floating on the horizon.
Our two bay mares are sleeping under it.
What matters least is what we don't have
in this moment, anything withheld pales
in waves rising from those two black pots.

THE BLACK DOOR IN *ARNAUDVILLE*

for Gloria Fiero

It might be what you don't see that most pleases
in this scene. There are possible banks everywhere
in this thick expanse of lively grassland. Water teases
a presence here and storms embed themselves in the charged air.

Beyond the darkest trees on the horizon whole families
may be filling sacks with choupique or handfishing for turtles.
Lovers could settle in away from us in that little cluster of trees

near the barn. But these are passing things. They startle
no one, mere skitterings to circumvent the black door of mysteries
opening the rusty tin-covered, white pyramid amidst all the marbled

life teeming here, a grave opening defying opening. No one sees
anything discernible beyond this dark plane. There is something there
we think or hope, but it invites nothing we can easily take comfort in, frees
nothing. Yet, it is the painter's gift to us, something the landscape has to bear.

From *Holding the Notes*

Forthcoming, 2011

(with special permission from Chicory Bloom Press)

"OF MEN AND RIVERS"

for Ernest J. Gaines

They used to catch fish out the river
and eat the fish and put the bones back.
They used to say, "Go back and be fish again."
— Jane Pittman

What he thinks of when he goes to the river
is not always what to take from it. Sometimes
it is what to put back that brings him there.
One day it will be the memory of all the lines

making catenaries on the surface of the water,
sometimes it will be the fish those lines brought in,
sometimes it will be the memory of all the quarter

residents and how they still live in him, old winds
the people gone before him ride on: aunts and daughters,
uncles and cousins shedding their troubles and their sins,

a brother dancing in the air above him, just a sliver
of memory but enough to keep him in the rhymes
of who he is and who they are and how to put them where
they belong as he lowers the bones of the fishes, spine and slime

and all, into the waters they came from. He knows the giver
must pay for what is given. He knows that all those times
he made those stories he lived them, how Jefferson quivered
before he could stand, how Tante Lou and Miss Emma saw crimes

and turned them back as much as they could with what they bartered.
He knows how Jimmy came to life and how he died. He begins
to see again at the water's edge. He knows again Big Laura's slaughter

and how to put it back. Here he can hear Reese Spooner talk again
on the back steps and he can hear his Aunt Augusteen ordering
the world she lived in with an open heart. The world does not spin

wildly when he comes back here. What Vivian needs he can give her
here, what drives Marcus he can say. The raw world and the grime
that comes from living in it is bearable at the water's edge it seems here
to him. The day, the year and everything in them witness to the Prime.

© Philip Gould

DARRELL BOURQUE is Professor Emeritus in English and Interdisciplinary Humanities from the University of Louisiana at Lafayette. Previous to *In Ordinary Light* he authored the following books of poems: *Plainsongs* (1994), *The Doors between Us* (1997), *Burnt Water Suite* (1999), *The Blue Boat* (2004), and *Call and Response: Conversations in Verse,* with Jack B. Bedell, (2009). In 2009 he directed the Imagining Lincoln: Louisiana Poetry Project as part of Louisiana and the nation's observance of the Abraham Lincoln Bicentennial. He lives in rural St. Landry Parish with his wife Karen who is a glass artist. *Holding the Notes,* a chapbook commissioned by Chicory Bloom Press, will be published in 2011. He served as Louisiana Poet Laureate during 2007 and 2008 and was reappointed to serve from 2009 to 2011.

UNIVERSITY OF LOUISIANA AT LAFAYETTE PRESS

LOUISIANA WRITERS SERIES

The Louisiana Writers Series is dedicated to publishing works that present Louisiana's diverse creative and cultural heritage. The series includes poetry, short stories, essays, creative nonfiction, and novels.

BOOKS IN THE LOUISIANA WRITERS SERIES:

The Blue Boat by Darrell Bourque (out of print)
Amid the Swirling Ghosts by William Caverlee
Local Hope by Jack Heflin
New Orleans: What Can't Be Lost edited by Lee Barclay
In Ordinary Light by Darrell Bourque

FOR MORE INFORMATION VISIT:

WWW.ULPRESS.ORG